MATH

HACK

SECRETS

MATH HACK SECRETS

*Level Up to Keep More
of Your Money*

SUZETTE T WHEELER, MBA

MATH
HACK
SECRETS

Cover Design: ebooklaunch.com
Editing: Heidi Scott Giusto, PhD
Book Design and Typesetting: Kerry Ellis
Author Photography: Connie McBeath

Published by Kind Society Press

The text type was set in Minion Pro

ISBN: 979-8-9906568-2-6 *(E-book)*
ISBN: 979-8-9906568-0-2 *(Paperback)*
ISBN: 979-8-9906568-1-9 *(Hardcover)*

Library of Congress Control Number: 2024916311

WWW.SUZETTETWHEELER.COM

Acknowledgements

This book was written as a thank you to my greatest math teacher, my father Tom Wheeler. With his instruction and guidance in math, I mastered math sufficiently well to achieve great accomplishments in my career and life.

I would also like to acknowledge my sister, Michele, a life-long math hack. Her ability to teach me math in a simple way not only helped me understand it better but also inspired me to pursue a math-based career.

Contents

How to Use This Book

"I'm redefining 'math' as a tool to use to save money."

-Suzette T Wheeler

We all know someone who says they hate math. Some people can relate to a popular song written by Jimmy Buffett called *"Math Suks"*. However, even if you hate math, understanding the basics and getting over your distaste can help you make good decisions and save money.

Understanding basic math is the single most powerful tool you can use to make excellent decisions for yourself and your family, too. This book offers the refresher on basic math that you might not want to admit you need. But once you learn to evaluate the prices of items you're buying, you can save thousands of dollars per year!

Why is math hard for some people? Many of you never learned or mastered the basics from multiplication tables to percentages. As a result, everything is more difficult as an adult because you don't have the solid math foundation that is needed to help make the best financial decisions.

In many instances, children are not taught why math is important. This often leads to poor math skills and financial struggles.

> **❝** When people talk about learning
> financial literacy skills, they are
> referring to understanding how to
> use simple math techniques to
> make better spending and saving
> decisions. **❞**

According to the United States Consumer Report, approximately 63% of adults in the U.S. are living paycheck to paycheck. While wages, inflation, and the cost of living are key factors, many people also lack basic budgeting and math skills that could save them from this stressful living situation.

Why is math worth learning? The biggest reason is that you can be in the driver's seat of your finances! Learning math ensures that you don't pay too much and allows you to keep the money in *your* pocket, rather than someone else's. You can level up your math skills by learning how to use simple math to make good purchasing decisions. In addition, by studying how to level up your math skills and do basic calculations, you can avoid being *"taken"* by others. There are some unscrupulous people who want to take advantage of you to their financial benefit. They are hoping that you are not good at math. They may try to convince you to pay MORE for a car, mortgage, or other expensive things. However, becoming skilled at the math in this book will help you calculate the best prices to find the best deals.

Reading this refresher math book will not only help you make better decisions about spending your money wisely but also discover how math can help you achieve more financial freedom in life. Often, we hear financial planners, real estate agents, and social media personalities say to us, *"Invest in a 401(k)! Invest in real estate and make passive income! Invest in stocks or bonds or invest in a financial program that will teach you how to invest in homes or stocks!"*

Those promises sound appealing, but if you don't fully understand math, it will be difficult to determine if you made a wise decision investing in these assets. Most likely, you will rely on these financial planners, real estate agents, and self-described gurus to tell you that you are making a good investment. Is that the best plan? I don't think so.

> 66 This book offers the refresher on basic math that you might not want to admit you need. 99

Some people who love math have said it gives them a competitive edge in business. They provide financial services by being a stockbroker, lender, Certified Professional Accountant *(CPA)*, or a commercial real estate broker, like me. Their financial careers depend on their ability to provide good financial advice. They are constantly using math to help their clients make good decisions.

People in other professions from nurses, radiologists, engineers, and architects use math for more scientific problem solving. They have had to develop solid math skills in order to take exams, complete their professional training, and ultimately work in these technical fields.

Throughout my career, I've seen how math calculations can result in huge financial savings. Having worked as a financial analyst in local government for twenty-six years, I did the math and developed new ways of doing business. The new business methods saved the government millions of dollars per year in cost savings.

> **❝❝ Understanding basic math can be the single most powerful tool to make excellent decisions for yourself and your family, too. ❞❞**

When you spend money each week on basic items like groceries, transportation, and other things, are you getting the best deal? This book provides practical guidance on how to spend money wisely in all types of experiences: buying groceries, purchasing a car, renting or buying a home, choosing a credit card, dining out, and budgeting expenses like holiday gift-buying and vacations. You may see things that you need on sale in stores. Are these items a good deal? You can do quick math to find out the actual cost and determine whether it's a good deal.

What do we do with the money we save by choosing the best deal? We can put that money away for holiday shopping, vacations, growing a savings account, and buying a car or a home! Getting in the habit of doing the math every day for things you buy will save you money that you can then deposit into a savings account or spend on higher-ticket purchases.

I have written this book so that everyone – from teens to adults - can use math to help find better deals in daily life and make smarter financial decisions. I am sharing my math hack secrets to help those who want to be more successful in their *"money keeping"* journey.

Not everyone grew up with parents who required their children to excel in math like mine did. But it's not too late! You can take simple steps today to start using math to save money!

This book was written for everyone who wants to succeed in life and build financial security by learning math and applying it to everyday life.

To use the book, I recommend reading each chapter and trying the word problems. If you already know the basic math and want to learn the financial math in later chapters, skip directly to those chapters.

Read the chapters that help you with problems you have now. You can also keep the book handy to refresh your knowledge as you encounter math in your daily life. This book allows you to focus on the topics most beneficial for you. You can skip chapters about information that you already know. Still, I recommend reading the chapters that you believe you know because they may reveal new nuggets of information.

Although this book covers everyday math that helps us make good decisions, it does not explore geometry, trigonometry, complex algebra, or calculus. Most daily math that you will use involves basic addition, subtraction, multiplication, and division.

Assumptions

When doing the math in the book, we assume that sales tax is not included. In Chapters 6 and 8, we will add sales tax to the purchase price.

Sales tax added to the purchase price will equal the total price paid for the item.

We will generally check our answers to the problems. I call it a *"sniff test."* You do the *"sniff test"* to check your numbers to make sure your math answers are approximately correct. If you get in the habit of doing this, you can feel confident about your math calculations no matter who questions whether your answers are correct. For example, you calculate your portion of a restaurant bill, but it seems unusually high based on what you ate. This probably indicates an error was made when adding up the bill – it doesn't pass the sniff test. We'll do this sniff test throughout the book on practice word problems.

Review: Basic Math Symbols

When you see a plus sign *(+)*, it means you will add the numbers in a row or column. If you see a minus *(-)* sign, that is the symbol for subtraction to subtract two numbers.

When you see a multiplication problem or are writing one *(you may hear the word **"times,"** which means you are multiplying two numbers)*, it may look like one of these below:

6 * 5 = 30 *(The asterisk means multiply, or 6 times 5 or multiply 6 by 5)*

6 X 5 = 30 *(The large X means multiply, and that 6 times 5 equals 30)*

6 / 2 = 3   *(The forward slash means 6 divided by 2)*

6 ÷ 2 = 3   *(The line with two dots means divide 6 by 2)*

If you master the concepts in this book, you will be sure to save thousands of dollars with your future purchases. Let's get started!

Chapter 1

Start Your Money Saving Journey

"I do the very best I know how – the very best I can;
and I mean to keep on doing so until the end."

-Abraham Lincoln

I was sitting in math class in fourth grade, and I was lost. The teacher had assigned us seats based on our last names. I was sitting in the back of the room with the other *"T through W"* last names. The kids with an *"A"* last name sat in front. They were lucky, I thought. They could see and hear the teacher and not be distracted by kids in front of them who were talking to each other and throwing things at each other. I was luckier than Tracey. Her last name started with a *"Z,"* so she was always in the last seat in the back row.

I had barely passed third grade math the prior year. In third grade, we had to memorize multiplication tables *(also known as the times tables)*. But fourth grade math was multiplication and division on steroids! 456 X 520 and 10,200 divided by 50!

In class, the fourth-grade teacher put a new chart on the wall at the beginning of the school year. The chart looked like a 10 X 30 grid. Each student's name was written on the horizontal axis, and their progress in completing a math packet group on the vertical axis. There were thirty students in my class.

Every time a student would complete a set of ten math packets, which was a math packet group, they would receive a gold star by their name in a box on the chart. In my class, the teacher placed a gold star on the board in the boxes by the child's name to show progress. The students in my class were very competitive and smart, and I saw a lot of gold stars in each row for most of the students. It seemed like every day, I heard the teacher say, **"She earned a gold star for that one."** See the chart in Figure 1-1.

Figure 1.1

	Math Packet Group 1	2	3	4	5	6	7	8	9	10
Judy	★									
Amber	★	★								
Michael	★	★	★	★						

I had no gold stars in my boxes on the chart. My boxes were empty. Other kids asked why I had empty boxes with no stars on the board. I said, **"Because I hate math."** Well, that didn't go over well with the teacher, who overheard what I said, threw up her arms in frustration, and frantically scribbled a note to my parents and handed it to me. I had to carry it home in shame.

I almost lost the note on the side of the road walking home... but decided I would be busted if I didn't bring it home! The note said, **"Suzette is flunking math. Please help!"**

My mom and dad were *so angry* with me when they read the note and saw my current grade in math: a big fat F. I was failing math! They grounded me and didn't let me go outside to play until I brought my grade up to an A. I learned that day that being good at math was the holy grail for my family. Thou shalt know math! Who knew?

To remedy my failing math grade, my dad came up with an idea. He told me that I would complete one math packet per day. Wow! A math packet had 10 pages in the packet and 20 math problems per page which equaled 120 math problems to do per day! Gulp, I had to solve 120 math problems every day. I lamented that my bike and skateboard would be sitting in the corner for a while.

The math problems in the packets were complex multiplication problems, like 234 X 498, and complex division problems, like 56,900 divided by 15. The packets also included word problems. We couldn't use calculators. We had to do the math by hand and show our work on the homework sheets.

I had a lot of math homework to complete each night. I would start solving the math problems on the worksheets at 2:00 p.m. when I got home. To finish the problems, I spent many hours in the afternoon working through them.

Under my father's close watch, I completed one packet each night. After I completed 10 packets, the teacher added one gold star on the board by my name.

I hated doing the math packets each night. One afternoon, my dad asked my sister and me to pick up the dog poop that our family dog had deposited in the backyard. My sister and I called it the *"poop patrol."* I tried to sneak out of the house to do poop patrol rather than do the boring math homework. My dad promptly noticed and asked me to finish my math problems first. I hated poop patrol, but I hated math problems more!

My mom also helped me with math during this time. She showed me tricks to figure out how to solve the problems, such as reading a math word problem and solving it by converting the words into math symbols *(X / + -)*. She also showed me how to solve complex math problems by breaking down the problem into smaller parts. This was very helpful to me to make math easier to understand and do. I will show you the tricks I learned from her in Chapter 2.

By the end of May of fourth grade, I had completed all 10 sets of 10 packets, which was 100 packets in all, 120 questions per packet, which meant I solved 100 X 120 = 12,000 math problems by the end of the year! I started the packets in January and finished in May, which meant I worked 100 days on math packets.

My parents were proud that finally, I filled out the chart with gold stars. I didn't know it at the time, but the 12,000 math problems put me ahead of most of the class. This advantage helped me move ahead in math for the rest of my time through school, college, and a successful career in finance. Why did this help? Learning math provided a positive momentum for me to continue to learn math and not fear it or hate it.

★ **Math Hack Secret** ★

If we don't use math every day, we can end up with less of our hard-earned money because we didn't find the best deal.

Everything in Life is a Math Problem to Solve

If someone asks you a question about your money, bills, financial investments, or home, then it likely involves solving a math problem. When you walk into a grocery store and choose one item to buy over another, you are using simple math to choose the best deal. If we don't use math every day, we can end up with less of our hard-earned money because we didn't find the best deal.

We see opportunities to buy things and determine how much it really costs all the time. It's important to know if you can afford to buy something, or whether it's a good deal and is worth buying at the time. When you compare prices and choose the best deal, you can start a Money Keeping Journal to record your hard-earned savings.

Create a Money Keeping Journal

How do you know how much you save by doing math? Simply use a Money Keeping Journal. I call it a Money Keeping Journal because it is a place where you can write about the money that you are keeping, rather than spending. As you read this book, you will start finding better prices and spending less money on things you need. I developed the Money Keeping Journal for you to keep track of your savings. Why? As you save money by comparing prices and choosing products wisely, your Money Keeping Journal will contain the savings amount that you can deposit in your bank account for use later.

Your Money Keeping Journal can be a notebook, the Apple Notes app or Google Keep app on your smart phone, or another app. To make it clear and readable if you use a notebook, I suggest you design the journal with the columns below in Figure 1.2. This form is also located in Appendix B.

Figure 1.2

Money Keeping Journal for _____						
Date	Store Name	Item Purchased	Reg. Price	My Price	Savings	Where Saved Money Deposited

Money Keeping Journal for – Enter or write your name in the box.

Date – The date you made the purchase.

Store Name – The place where you bought the item or service.

Item – What you bought.

Reg. Price – The regular price of the item.

My Price – The price you paid for the item.

Savings – The Reg. Price minus My Price. This reveals the amount you saved when you bought the item or service.

Where Savings Deposited – When you save money on a purchase, deposit the money you saved into a savings account or money market account, not a checking account. Why? It's too easy to spend your savings if it's deposited into a checking account. You can keep more of your savings by placing the money in an account that is not linked to a checking account for withdrawals.

This recordkeeping strategy works by filling in the Money Keeping Journal with numbers and the amount of savings. Even if you use a credit card for the purchase, move the savings you calculated from checking to your savings account each day or at least once a week. If you use a debit card that is attached to your checking account, move the money you saved from checking to savings. Using cash? Set aside the money you saved, and deposit it into your savings account when you have a chance. Remove the cash from your wallet and place it in an envelope that you put away. Deposit the money in the envelope into your savings account at least once a month.

You will see how you can save on purchases in almost every chapter of the book, especially Chapter 10, which explains how your savings can improve your life. Watch your savings grow as you make sound purchasing decisions that result in saving money.

Key Money-Saving Tips

1) Create a Money Keeping Journal to keep track of the money you saved by comparing prices and choosing the best option.

2) Open a separate savings account to deposit the money you've tracked in your Money Keeping Journal for purchases.

Chapter 2

Find Great Deals with Simple Math Tools

"Look before, or you'll find yourself behind."

–Benjamin Franklin

W hen I was seventeen-years-old, I decided to give up working in a hamburger restaurant, and work in a retail store where I could dress in nice clothes and help customers find new clothes every day. To work at a nice retail store, I needed a car to drive back and forth. The bicycle would not do. I looked for used cars and found a car dealer that offered a 5% discount on the purchase of a car for students. *How much was the discount in dollars*, I wondered.

Why are percentages *(often shortened to "percent")*, decimal, and fractions important to understand? You will convert fractions and percents into decimals, which can be used in very important transactions in life, such as buying a car, taking out a loan, or purchasing a home.

Definitions

Let's first explain the difference between **decimals**, **fractions**, and **percents**.

A **decimal** is a number that is preceded by a decimal point, like the number .60. Decimals that are less than one but greater than zero. We can describe it as 'point 60' or even '60 percent.' Percents are converted into decimals to solve math problems. Decimals are used in a math problem like this: .10 X 500 = 50. A decimal is another way of writing a percent. For example, 10 percent *(10%)* is the same as the decimal .10.

A **fraction** is defined as two numbers, a numerator *(top number)* and a denominator *(the bottom number)*. A fraction is a part of a whole number. It's less than one and greater than zero. The numerator is divided by the denominator in a fraction to get a decimal value. A fraction looks like this: 3/5. This fraction is read aloud as 'three fifths'. You use fractions when baking and cooking as well as when measuring spaces and objects. A fraction is another way to represent a percent. Sometimes you will see a sale that offers 1/3 off the regular price. I focus primarily on percents because that is what we see most often when we are shopping for something.

A **percent** is defined as a fraction or part of 100. An example of a percent is '20 percent' or 20%. Percents can be seen everywhere when buying items. For example, 20% off the shoes, or 50% off a subscription to a newspaper. Percents, when converted to decimals, are also often less than one but greater than zero, such as when an item is marked at a 50% discount, which means you'll pay half of the original price. Percent means divided by 100. For example, 25% = 25/100 = 0.25.

Back to Basics with Percents and Decimals

In elementary school, my math teacher taught me that percents can be converted to decimals. What does that mean? I thought.

Why are we converting percents to decimals? The kids had math problems like this:

What is the decimal equivalent to 10%?

I had no clue how to convert a percent to a decimal, or how they were used. I didn't know that I would be using percents and decimals every day to buy groceries, clothes, and basic items. Or that using decimals would help me quickly calculate a tip on a meal, sales tax, or interest on a loan.

To understand decimals, we first need to look at how large or small the numbers are, depending on where the decimal point is located. Numbers can grow smaller when we place numbers to the right of the decimal point. A number with a decimal point to the left of it is less than 1 but greater than zero. Zeros to the right of the decimal point make the number smaller. For example, in Figure 2.1:

Figure 2.1

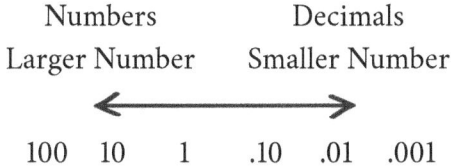

So, if a number has a decimal point (.) as the first character in the number, it's called a **decimal. Decimals** are less than one but greater than zero.

I remember the teacher saying, ***"To convert a percent to a decimal, you move the decimal point two places to the left."*** To make a percent into a decimal, we divide by 100.

10/100 = .10 which is 10%.

To move the decimal place on a percent, like 10%, we first start with the 10 of the 10 percent.

10 ⟵ move the decimal place two places to the left so that 10 looks like .10.

10% becomes .10.

Let's try 50%:

50% - Move decimal two spaces to the left to convert a percent to a decimal.

50.   this is the movement of the decimal point to the left two places.

.50 - 50% becomes .50.

You can convert decimals to percents the same way, except move the decimal to the *right* two spaces.

.60 is also equal to 60%

The decimal moved two spaces to the right, for the .60 decimal to become 60 percent.

> 66 The only difference between a percent and a decimal is moving the decimal point two spaces to the left. 99

For most of your math problems, you will be using decimals and fractions. It's important to know how to convert a percent to a decimal. You will do it for most math you solve in everyday life. If we don't convert a percent to a decimal first before trying to solve a math problem, then we can't solve the math problem. I call it *"move two."* A percentage becomes a decimal by moving the decimal point two places to the left.

Have you noticed there is no percent *(%)* button on most calculators? It's not there because the calculator wants you to use a decimal to calculate a math problem, not a percent.

Rounding Up and Down

When you are using decimals, it will be easier to do basic math if you round your decimal up or down to a two-digit number, to make the math easier to do. If you're dividing something on a calculator, and the answer extends to many decimal points, round it to two-digit numbers.

For example, 100 divided by 3 is a math problem. Let's say that three men have decided to divide $100 among them. What is $100 divided by three men? The answer is $33.33333. Each man receives $33.3333 of the money. To make this answer make sense, we need to round the number down to a two-digit decimal, so it becomes $33.33. Each man receives $33.33 which makes it much easier to split the money, right?

The rules to round up or down work are like this:

If a number is 1 – 4, round the number down. If a number is 5 through 9, round the number up.

Let's put this into practice. If you want to use a decimal and the decimal you calculate is .345, and you want to use a two-digit decimal, your three-digit decimal will have to be rounded up or down to make it a two-digit decimal. How do we get rid of the third number on the right and round it up to be a two-digit decimal? We look at the third number on the right, which is 5.

As discussed earlier, we know that a 5 rounds up, so it will round up the number next to it – i.e., the 4. The 4 now becomes a 5 because it's rounded up by the 5. Add 1 to the 4 in the hundredths place to round it up to 5. So, the new two-digit decimal is now .35. In short:

the 5 goes away and increases the 4 to a 5. Decimals can be rounded up and down and the number on the right side, in this case the 5, can be deleted and the remaining numbers round up or down.

.345 rounds up to become .35.

Let's look at another example: We have the number 452, the number of insulated cups in the warehouse. Your boss wants a rounded number to describe the insulated cups in general. What number should you give him? For whole numbers, we keep the total number of digits, in this case 3, and just round up or down the last number to the right. The last number to the right is 2. The number for 452 is rounded down because the 2 is the number on the right and it rounds down *(1 – 4 numbers round down)*. So, in rounded numbers, the warehouse has approximately 450 cups *(452 rounded down becomes 450)*.

The value of a number depends on the location of the decimal point. When the decimal point is to the left of the numbers, it means the number is less than one but greater than zero. See Figure 2.2 below.

Figure 2.2

1	One
.10	One tenth or 10 percent
.01	One one-hundredth or one percent
.001	One one-thousandth or one tenth of one percent
.0001	One hundred thousandth or one hundredth of one percent

To see how the decimals shown in Figure 2.2 work, let's do a quick math observation. Below is an example of how to determine the value of a decimal.

What number is smaller, .10 or .0001?

If our manager had $1 million dollars, and we could choose which decimal amount above *(.10 or .0001)* to multiply by the $1 million, and the resulting number would be our take home bonus paycheck, which number would you choose?

Let's try .10 which is 10%. Use .10 to multiply by $1,000,000:

$1,000,000 X .10 = $100,000

$100,000 is the bonus paycheck you would take home.

Let's compare the answer $100,000 to the answer using .0001 *(one-one hundredth of one percent)* to multiply by $1,000,000:

$1,000,000 X .0001 = $1,000

$1,000 is the bonus paycheck you would take home.

Which bonus paycheck would you rather have, $100,000 or $1,000? Of course, you would choose .10, which gives a bonus of $100,000, rather than .0001, which gives a bonus of $1,000. Why? Because .10 converts to a percentage of 10% and .0001 converts to a percentage of .01%.

Another math skill we can learn is how to set up a math problem by converting words in the math problem to math symbols.

Tricks to Working with Word Problems

The part of math that was the most difficult for me were the **"word problems."** Word problems are math exercises written as a question. You might recall in elementary school having to find out how many muffins were left after Sam ate six, for instance. Students had to find an answer by figuring out how to solve the problem through math. As a child, I didn't know *why* we needed to learn how to solve word problems. I didn't care how many muffins were left.

Word problems look like this:

Amy has $50 in cash in her pocket. She goes to the store to buy a shirt. The shirt she likes is $60, and the store is offering a 20% discount if she buys it today. She knows that to find the discount, she will be taking 20% off the shirt price, which will equal the discount. Then she will subtract the discount from the shirt price to get the sale price. How much is the shirt on sale?

Solve it as $60 X .20 *(20% discount)* = $12 discount off the price of the shirt.

It will be a word problem written as something like the following: What is 20% of $60?

$60 - $12 discount = $48 = the sale price of the shirt

This will be a simplified word problem written as: What is the sale price of the shirt if we deduct $12 from the shirt price?

Sales tax is not added to this word problem to make it simple to understand. In Chapters 6 and 8 we will add sales tax to the purchase price.

How does this help us in real life? When we are looking for good deals to buy at the store, knowing how to determine if a particular item is a deal comes in handy!

Mom's Math Tricks to Solve Word Problems: Look for Of, Is, and From

My mom sat down with me as I struggled to learn how to solve word problems. She explained the three simple steps to solve a word problem. She also said there are three words that convert to math symbols: **Of, Is,** and **From.** The three steps are shown below:

A. Break down the word problem into numbers and math symbols.

B. Convert the words, *of, is,* and *from* into math symbols.

C. Solve the math problem.

"OF" means you will be <u>multiplying</u> the numbers next to the **"OF."**

When you see **"OF"** in a word problem or hear the word OF, it means you will be <u>multiplying</u> *(using the symbols X or *)* the two numbers.

In the example above, Amy wants to know the sale discount amount. She is calculating 20% OF $60. OF means multiply, so the math problem looks like this:

$60 X 20% = discount amount.

"IS" means the <u>equal sign</u> *(=)*.

In the example above *(what is 20% of $60?)* IS means equal *(=)* and OF means multiply, so the problem looks like this:

20% X $60 =

If a word problem doesn't specifically say the word *"IS,"* that's okay. You will likely be writing the equal sign *(=)* as part of your work to solve the problem.

Notice that we saw the math problem written two ways: 20% of 60 and 60 X 20%. Both ways are correct.

"FROM" means you will be <u>subtracting</u> *(-)* the numbers.

An example of using the word FROM: 40 from 100 is 60.

The math equation looks like: 100 – 40 = 60.

★ **Math Hack Secret** ★

Turning Words into Math Symbols

"OF" means you will be <u>multiplying</u> the numbers next to the *"OF."*

"IS" means the equal sign *(=).*

"FROM" means you will be <u>subtracting</u> *(-)* the numbers.

Let's convert words into a math problem. Here is an example of a word problem:

Jim went to the store to buy a garden blower machine so he could blow the leaves in his yard into big piles, which would be easier for him to pick up. He sees a fabulous blower for $200. The salesman in the store told him that he could get a great deal on the blower; it's currently on sale for 60% off. Jim has shopped around and knows blowers are usually sold for around $200. Jim knows if he hired someone, the person would charge $50 to blow leaves. Jim decided he wanted to do the work and not pay for someone every time the leaves needed to be cleaned up. How much will Jim spend to buy a blower?

Let's figure out how much Jim can save and the price of the blower at the new sales price.

Ask these questions:

1) What is the discount amount that Jim will receive, or what is 60% of 200?

2) What is the new sales price of the blower machine with the 60% discount? What is $200 minus the discount amount?

Let's solve it to find the sale price of the blower.

IS means the equal sign (=), so the first thing we do is write the equal sign (=). So, it looks like this:

Sixty percent of 200 is written as: 60% of 200 is X, or 60% X 200 = X. X is the number we are trying to solve, in this case the discount amount.

Next, we change the 60 percent to a number we can use to solve the problem. We must change it to a decimal from a percentage, so we move the decimal point to the left two places for the two numbers.

Sixty percent becomes .60.

After we change a percent to a decimal, we can use it to calculate a math problem.

60% of $200 = X
60% is .60
Of means multiply *(X)*
.60 **X** 200 = $120

Jim will save $120 off the price of the blower. But what is the new sales price of the blower?

Another way to say it is 'What is $120 *from* $200?' or 'What is the full price of the blower minus the discount?'

$200 *(full price)* - $120 *(discount)* = $80. $80 is the sales price of the blower. Jim is excited and buys the blower for $80 at 60% off.

Tips and Tricks to Calculate the Sale Price

An easy way to figure out the sales price: If Jim is getting 60% off, that means he is only paying 40% of the regular price. So, to quickly calculate his new price, multiply 40% or .40 times the full price, $200, to get the new sales price. 40% X $200 = $80.

What happens if you see 200%? What does it mean and how do we solve it? We may hear a news blast saying the price of widgets will increase by 200% next year. The price of widgets currently is $10 each. We want to know the price for next year. To do the math, you move the decimal 2 places to the left, and the decimal number becomes 2.00. What does 200% really mean? It means that a number is multiplied by 2, which doubles the number. For example, the widget is currently $10, and we want to multiply it by 200%. 200% of 10 converts to 2 X 10 which equals 20. So, widgets will be priced at $20 next year if the price increases by 200%. It also works if you use 300%. We want to know what 300% of 10 is. So, we convert 300% to 3 then multiply with 10 to get 30 *(3X10=30)*.

Word Problems Using Fractions and Division

A. We want to double the fraction of 3/4 *(three fourths)*. We have a cookie recipe that uses 3/4 cups of packed brown sugar. We know the family and friends each want a bag of our cookies. So, we must double the recipe to have enough cookies to give out. How much brown sugar do we need? Hint: We need to multiply 3/4 by 2.

B. We use five computer components per day to fix computers in our shop. How many days will the computer component inventory last if we have 600 components currently in inventory? Hint: What is 600 divided by 5?

C. The store is selling cell phones for 1/3 off, if we buy it today. The regular price of the phone is $800. How much is the cell phone's sales price with the one-third discount? Hint: What is one third of $800?

How to Solve These Word Problems

A. As a reminder, a fraction is defined as two numbers: a numerator *(the top number)* and a denominator *(the bottom number)*. For the first math problem, doubling 3/4 will be 3/4 X 2. The best way to multiply fractions is to line them up, numerator on the top and denominator on the bottom. Do the same with the 2. *(Any whole number is the number over one, so 2 is actually 2/1.)*

$$\frac{3 \text{ X } 2}{4 \text{ X } 1} = \frac{6}{4}$$

The answer is 6/4. But 6/4 is not a value on a baking measuring cup. How do we make 6/4 a number we can use? As a refresher, the line that divides the numbers is called the divider line and it tells us to divide the numbers. So, we divide six by four. Or another way to say it is 4 divided into 6. When you see the divider line, you will be dividing the bottom number into the top number.

```
       1.5
  4 | 6
      4
      2 0
      2 0
        0
```

The answer is 1.5, which means that 3/4 doubled is 1.5 or one-and-a-half. We will need one-and-a-half cups of packed brown sugar in the recipe to double that ingredient in the cookies. All the rest of the ingredients will be doubled as well in order to follow the cookie recipe.

B. How many days will our inventory last if we have 600 parts and use 5 parts per day?

What is 600 divided by 5? Or another way to say it is 'What is 5 divided into 600?' Using 5 parts a day, we want to solve for the number of days the supply of parts will last.

The problem is set up like this if you calculate it manually.

```
  5 | 600
```

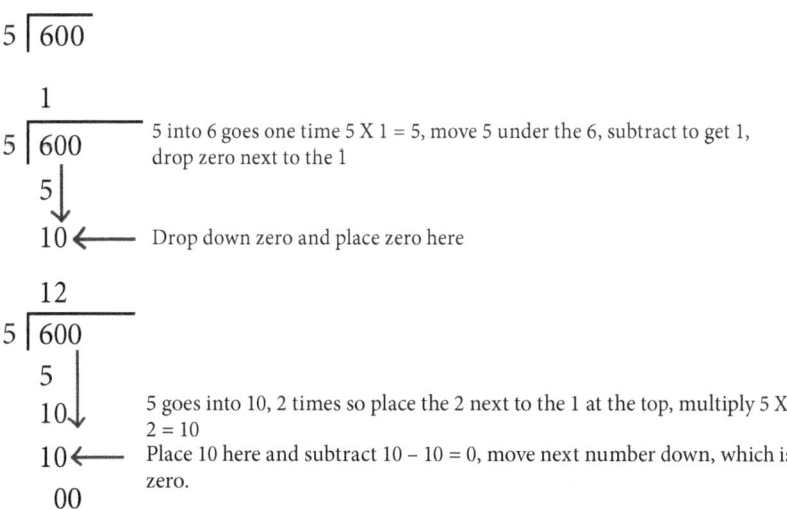

```
      1
  5 | 600      5 into 6 goes one time 5 X 1 = 5, move 5 under the 6, subtract to get 1,
      5        drop zero next to the 1
      ↓
     10 ←————— Drop down zero and place zero here

     12
  5 | 600
      5
     10 ↓      5 goes into 10, 2 times so place the 2 next to the 1 at the top, multiply 5 X
     10 ←————  2 = 10
     00        Place 10 here and subtract 10 – 10 = 0, move next number down, which is
               zero.
```

```
    120
   ─────
 5 │ 600
    5
    10
    10
    00  ←─── 5 into 0 is 0, so place the zero as the third number on the top, resulting in
              120 as the answer.
```

The answer is 120. The parts supply will last 120 days if we use 5 parts per day to fix computers.

The problem can also be solved when you use the calculator and enter the numbers:

Type in 600

Tap the divided by button *(÷)*

Type 5

Tap enter or the *(=)* button

The number on the screen should be 120.

C. To calculate 1/3 of 800, we need to know how 1/3 converts to a decimal, so we can use the decimal to multiply with 800 to find the discounted amount.

1/3 is rounded to .33 in decimal form. You can check this on your calculator.

Type in 1

Tap the divided by button *(÷)*

Type in 3

Tap enter or the *(=)* button

Your answer will be .3333. It's good to memorize that 1/3 is actually .33.

Let's round the decimal down to .33. It's best to use decimals with two digits for basic math problems.

Multiply 800 by .33 *(the discounted decimal value)* = $264. $264 is the amount of the discount of the $800 price. Now we can do the math to find the sale price of the phone.

We subtract the discount of $264 from $800, to get the new discounted sales price, $536 *($800 – $264 = $536).*

Another quick way to solve this problem is to use the discount of 33% and subtract it from 100% to get 67%. One hundred percent price minus 33% discount is 67% for the new discounted price. Sixty-seven percent converts to .67 times $800 is .67 X $800 = $536, the sales price of the phone.

To summarize the math problems we solved above, doing the math helped us figure out how to double a recipe, determine how long inventory will last, and determine how much a discount is worth for a cell phone, and what the new price is. Multiplication is very powerful and converting percents to decimals before you solve the problem will give you the power to know the true price of sale items.

For additional problems to solve to practice your math skills, try these exercises below:

1) Visit a store or go online and look for a jacket or coat that is on sale. Find the percent off that the company is offering. Do the multiplication to find out what the discount amount is. Do the subtraction *(full price minus the discount)* to figure out the sales price of the item. This works better if you go into a store because most of the time the store does not show the new sales price, only the discount percentage.

2) Visit a computer store. Look for a computer on sale and find one that is full price. Study the options available on each

computer. Figure out the discount and the sales price of the sale computer versus the full priced one. Ask yourself if the sale computer offers as much or more features than the full priced computer. Is the computer worth buying now or will there be another sale later that aligns with the money you will be able to save to buy it later with cash? Compare full priced items to items on sale. How much do you save by buying the item on sale and is it worth the savings?

Key Money-Saving Tips

1) To solve a problem when an item is on sale for a percent off, e.g., 20%, we must first convert the 20% to a decimal and then use multiplication to solve the problem.

2) Round up and down to make multiplication easier for decimal numbers: if the last digit is 4 or less, round down. If the number is 5 or more, round up.

3) When dividing a large number by another large number, divide from the left to the right side, under the divider line.

Chapter 3

Add and Subtract Your Way to Savings

"Beware of little expenses; a small leak will sink a great ship."

—Benjamin Franklin

My mom and dad knew that having a good education was the ticket to moving up and obtaining a better economic position in the United States. Their goal was to achieve a better financial position than their parents *(my grandparents)*. They always said to their children, ***"We want you to do better financially than we did. We want you to excel beyond what we have done and become wealthier than we have achieved."*** They told us we could do anything we dreamed of and achieve more in life than them. My mom called it, ***"Pulling yourself up by your bootstraps."*** My parents consistently emphasized the importance of our education, especially math.

I don't remember learning that addition and subtraction was so important in school. I used my fingers a lot to add and subtract numbers. Sometimes, I used my toes to count, too. Who knew as a kid that as an adult we would be using addition and subtraction to split bills with other people for food, lodging, or trips? I was learning how to add and subtract, rather than *why* it was valuable to learn to add and subtract numbers. Without understanding *"why,"* I never fully understood the math lessons and struggled to remember them.

As I became an adult, however, I learned that addition and subtraction can be used every day in our lives to save money on purchases. I realized the importance of math—just like my parents had so many years before.

The basic math problems below demonstrate how to add and subtract numbers manually. Why do we do math problems this way? It helps us memorize addition and subtraction, so we don't need to rely on a calculator for every math or word problem we encounter daily.

Basic Math: Add and Subtract from Right to Left in the Math Problem

I remember my mom showing me the way to add and subtract large math problems. She said to solve math problems, we should add or subtract from the right column of the math problem and move to the next left column.

An example of a subtraction math problem is:

$$\begin{array}{r} 1550 \\ -\ 100 \\ \hline \end{array}$$

We can do math problems by <u>adding and subtracting from the right side of the math problem to the left side</u>.

We work on the problem right to left using the columns.

In column 1, zero minus zero is zero. Place the zero below the two zeros in the answer column.

```
      ↓column 1
  1550
−  100
 ─────
     0
```

Move to the next column to the left. Five minus 0 is 5. Place the 5 in the answer column under the 5 and 0.

```
      ↓column 2
  1550
−  100
 ─────
    50
```

Move to the next column to the left. Five minus 1 is 4. Place the 4 in the answer column under the 5 and 1.

```
     ↓column 3
  1550
−  100
 ─────
   450
```

Move to the next column to the left. One minus the blank is 1. The blank space is actually a 0. So, the number can be written as 0100. Place the 1 in the answer column under the 1 and blank.

```
     ↓column 4
  1550
−  100
 ─────
  1450
```
1450 - The answer to 1550 minus 100 is 1,450.

Let's look at a word problem and story and do subtraction to get the answer. Mabel has $4,567 in her money market bank account, and she wants to withdraw $380. How much money is left in her bank account after the withdrawal?

$4,567 − $380 = X *(X is the money left in her bank account)*

Let's find out how much money Mabel will have after she deducts $380 from her money market account:

$4,567 in her account currently
− 380 Minus the amount of money she is withdrawing

Work on the problem from right to left by columns.

Column 1 shows 7 minus 0 = 7

$$\downarrow$$

$$4567$$
$$-\ 380$$
$$\overline{7}$$

Now move to the next column, 6 minus 8. We can't have a negative number 6 − 8 = -2. To make a positive number we have to borrow from the next column over, the 5. 5 becomes 4 in the 3rd column and the 1 moves in front of the 6 making it 16. When you borrow a 1, you are actually borrowing 10 from the left column. So, 6 plus 10 equals 16 and now 8 can be subtracted from it. 16 minus 8 = 8. Write the 8 to the left of the 7.

$$\downarrow$$

$$4^1$$
$$4567$$
$$-\ 380$$
$$\overline{87}$$

Now we have two more columns to solve, the column starting with the new 4 and the left column with the 4. The new 4 minus 3 = 1, which goes into the next column at the bottom.

$$\downarrow$$
$$4^1$$
$$4567$$
$$-\ 380$$
$$\overline{187}$$

The last column to the left is 4 minus 0, because there is no number to subtract from it, so place the 4 in the most left column.

$$\downarrow 4^1$$
$$4567$$
$$-\ 380$$
$$\overline{4187}$$

The answer is $4,187. Mabel will have $4,187 after she withdraws $380 from her money market bank account.

Other ways to use math are when we are shopping for items.

Use Addition and Subtraction When Shopping at the Grocery Store

Create a Shopping List

Before you shop for groceries or make any shopping trip, prepare a shopping list beforehand. For grocery shopping, write down the items you have to buy for meals and for household needs. This list will help you refrain from buying items that you do not need. Write down the estimated price of each item and add it up to create a budget for the shopping trip.

Take the list with you to the store and shop only for items on the list. Do not allow yourself to buy items that are not on the list. Only buying items on the list will help you save money on the shopping trip and keep more of your money in your bank account. This can be a challenge, but it is worth the effort. To reward yourself for only buying items on the list, write down the item and the price of the item you did **not** buy in your money keeping journal. The costs of the items you don't buy are actually savings for you. You may add in these items on your next grocery shopping trip if they fit within your budget.

Comparing Similar Items

When shopping for groceries, look at every item you pick up to buy, and look at similar items on the shelf, and compare prices to find the less expensive item. For example, you decide to buy a can of corn you need for a recipe. The can of corn you are holding is a national brand and costs two dollars. On the shelf next to this can is a store brand can of corn. The store brand costs $1.50 per can.

What do you do?

Compare the number of ounces in each can. Make sure the number of ounces is the same for each one. Let's say each can contains 15 ounces.

Compare the price of the corn to each other. One can costs $2 and the other one costs $1.50. By doing quick math, you know that you would save fifty cents on your grocery bill if you bought the store brand.

Determine if the less expensive can of corn will work for your needs. Sometimes recipes will list the ingredients needed as national brand products. It's your choice to choose the product you need.

Choose the product that works for your needs and put it in your basket.

If you are buying the less expensive item, mark the savings in your Money Keeping Journal.

Look For Sales

Most likely, a grocery store will have advertised sales on various products. They may advertise the sales in a flyer available at the store, on-line or in a local newspaper. Look at the advertised sales to decide if the items on sale are products you want to buy for a meal in the near future.

If you are shopping in the store and see a sale on groceries, compare prices on the sale items with the regular priced items. Sometimes sale items do not cost less than the regular priced items. Do quick math to see if the sale is really the best deal. Following these steps will help you save money at the grocery store and other retailers where you shop.

Use Addition and Subtraction When Shopping: Buying Earrings at an Art Show

Let's see how we can save money on purchases that we buy in the marketplace. Let's go to an art show and look around for a gift for our friend.

We see some handmade earrings that would be a perfect gift for our friend.

The red pair of earrings cost $10, and the blue pair of earrings cost $20. You decide to buy the two pairs of earrings.

You hand the two pairs of earrings to the artist in the art booth. She says the total and amount due from you is $40. Is that correct? Should you question the total she said you owe? Definitely!

Let's add it up:

$10 red earrings
+ $20 blue earrings
$30 total for both pairs of earrings

Why is she asking you to pay $40 when the total cost of the earrings is $30? That is a good question to ask her. To save money and not pay too much, asking questions about the total is useful if it does not look correct.

You ask the artist about the difference in your expected total and the amount she wants to charge you. She looks at the bill and tells you she charged you $20 for each pair *($20 + $20 = $40)*, rather than $20 and $10. She sees she made an error, apologizes, and recalculates your bill to be $30.

It's important that you look at all the prices of items you put in your basket to buy. Especially in a grocery store, look at the prices listed on the shelf when you choose an item; either take notes or remember the sale price. When you arrive at the checkout counter, and the clerk is ringing up your order, watch the prices on the screen as the cashier is ringing up the items. Make sure you're seeing the correct price *(the price indicated on the shelf sign)* for the item. If the price doesn't look right, ask the clerk about it. Sometimes the staff who make price changes forget to change the price in the computer system. Therefore, the price is incorrect when it's rung up at the register.

A friend named Heidi was at the grocery store over Christmas and five produce items *(vegetables)* rang up differently at the cash register than they were advertised. The difference was about $20. Heidi chose the produce based on the clearly advertised sale price that had never been inputted into their system. She knew she had to double-check her prices at the register when she or the clerk was ringing up the prices. Heidi saved $20 by noticing the wrong prices and asking the clerk to fix the price problem.

We may know people who don't look at the price in the grocery store because they figure *"I need it, so it doesn't matter."* But that just means they are missing out on making better decisions and/or can't confirm what they are charged at the checkout counter is the advertised price.

Let's buy some books online. Let's say you want to buy two copies of a book titled *Math Hack Secrets*. You click on the order button to buy the two books, click on the check-out button, and the summary looks like this:

Math Hack Secrets	2 @ $28 = $56
Frank Knows His English	$15
Total:	$71

What happened? In your head, you are quickly adding up $28 + $28 for two books = $56.

Then you look at the total to see if it makes sense—you're doing the 'sniff test' mentioned earlier. You're expecting to see $56. However, the bill is $71. Ask yourself what changed to make the total cost more than expected. You look at the order and notice another book was added. What in the heck is the *Frank Knows His English* book doing in my order, you might wonder.

It seems you mistakenly ordered a different book you had been previously considering. By reviewing your order to make sure you have the right books in your cart before you pay and **using quick math to quickly add up the book costs in your head**, you can save money and avoid paying more than you want and getting items that you don't want. You can also save a headache by not having to return a book.

Let's look at this word problem below. You will find that when you solve a word problem like this one, you will be using addition, subtraction, and multiplication to solve everyday problems.

Field Trip to Tule Springs State Park: Creating a Budget

When I was a child, we took a trip to a large state park in Nevada called Tule Springs State Park.

I remember sitting on a school bus with a bunch of big kids, and they were singing a song they made up, *"Toot Toot to Tule Springs!"* as we drove along. All the windows of the bus were down, and a cool breeze was rushing through the bus. It smelled like a mix of the native creosote bush in the desert and body odor, from the older kids of course! I could hear the metal clanking and rattling from the underside of the bus as it hit potholes in the road. The teacher handed out a notebook and pencil to each student before we got off the bus at the park. We were asked to draw and write the names of animals and birds we saw. I was so excited to look for birds and animals and draw pictures of them. Unfortunately, we disturbed a beehive, which led to an unexpected math activity. Someone laid their blanket over a sprinkler box where the bees had made their home. The bees got mad and made a *"bee line drive"* at the kids. A lot of running around ensued as the bees chased the kids and adults! All I could hear was buzzing sounds and kids screaming as the bees descended upon them. I did a lot of math that day, counting bee stings on the other kids and myself.

As kids, we didn't think about how the trip was put together or the cost.

The teacher who coordinated the trip did though. The school received a grant from the government to pay for field trips to *"enlighten"* us about nature and our natural environment.

I'll make up a list of costs and how the teacher would have used math to make sure the trip cost was less than the grant amount which was her budget.

The teacher received a government grant in the amount of $200. We will set a budget that would be similar to today's prices, say $1,000.

The teacher created a budget for the $1,000 grant amount so it would pay for the cost of the trip. How did she set up the budget?

First, she **estimated expenses for the field trip**. She wrote a list of questions she had to answer to plug the numbers into her budget.

1) **How many chaperones and students were going on the trip?**

   She knew that twenty-four students wanted to go on the trip, and their parents signed field trip waivers so they could go.
   Five chaperones planned to go on the trip, too. The teacher was one of the chaperones.
   How many chaperones and students were going on the trip?
   Let's add it up: 24 students + 5 chaperones = 29. A total of 29 students and chaperones are going on the trip.

2) **How much does the school bus cost to transport the students and chaperones to the park and return to the school?**

   School bus cost: $400 per day including a driver. The driver would bring his own lunch on the trip. So, she did not have to budget for lunch for the driver.

3) **How much will lunch and water cost for twenty-nine people?**

   The box lunches for the students and chaperones are $10 each. Bottled water: 3 cases of bottled water – cost is $10 for each case. Each case had 24 bottles of water. The teacher was assuming that each person would drink at least two bottles of water during the trip.

The food budget looked like this:

24 students X $10 box lunch = $240
5 chaperones X $10 box lunch = $50
3 cases of water X $10 for each case = $30

4) **How much will the pencils and notebooks cost to buy for the
    students to use?**

First, let's find the price to pay for pencils and paper. One packet
of pencils contains 10 pencils. We have 24 students who need a
pencil. How many packets do we need for all the students? Well,
10 students will use the first packet, which has 10 pencils. Ten
more students will use the second packet. So, 10 + 10 = 20. Twenty
students can have a pencil if we buy two packets of pencils.

Are two packets enough pencils? No, four students don't have a
pencil. 24 students – 20 students who have a pencil = 4 students left.
So, we will add another packet of pencils for the last four students.

One way to do the math is to take 24 students divided by 10 pencils
per packet = 2.4 packets needed. Because pencils are sold in units
of ten, we need to buy a third packet, so everyone has a pencil.
We would have to buy three packets with a total of 30 pencils. A
pack of 10 pencils cost $3.

How much do we have to pay for pencils? We multiply $3 per pack
of pencils X 3 packs of pencils = $9.

Each notebook costs $3.00. 24 students will be given a notebook.
How much will 24 notebooks cost? We multiply 24 notebooks X
$3 per notebook = $72 for 24 notebooks.

All these costs look like a lot of information, but it's easy when
you break the costs into separate lines for the budget.

Now we have the dollar amounts for each expense and need to add all the expenses for the field trip:

Bus and bus driver	= $400
24 students X $10 box lunch	= $240
5 chaperones X $10 box lunch	= $50
3 cases of water X $10 for each case	= $30
3 pencil packets 3 X $3 each	= $9
24 notebooks 24 X $3	= $72
Total	= $801

Add up all the costs: $400 + $240 + $50 + $30 + $9 + $72 = $801

Does the $801 in expenses fit our budget of $1,000? Yes, it does!

They can now purchase the items and go on the field trip. Toot toot to Tule Springs!

You can use this type of budget exercise for countless activities. Budgeting for vacations or for holiday spending is very important and you can find more strategies in Chapter 10.

Bike Riding Adventure: Splitting the Expenses Between Two Friends

When groups of people go on trips out of town to another city or place, one traveler in a group may, for example, buy tickets for the group and another may buy a group dinner for the group. To make it fair for all, the group may decide to split the costs, so each person pays their fair share. This story is a bike riding story where we can do the math to make the costs fair to each person.

Two bicycle riding friends, Ellie and Suzette, decided to take a trip to Utah to ride the hills in Zion National Park. They stayed in a hotel nearby. Ellie paid for the hotel room in advance. The friends agreed to split the room charge. Suzette wanted to pay for her share of the room to Ellie before she left Utah. During the trip, Suzette bought drinks at a rest stop, and Ellie said she would reimburse Suzette for the drink that Suzette bought for Ellie. The purchases to split look like this:

> Ellie paid for the hotel room which cost $90 total.
> Suzette paid $10 for two drinks: Ellie's drink was $5, and Suzette's was $5.
> To reimburse Ellie for the room minus the cost that Suzette paid for Ellie's drink, what did Suzette pay Ellie to settle up the cost for the trip?

If they divide the room charge $90 by 2 for the two women to split, it's $45 each.

What about the drink? How does Suzette get paid for the drink she bought for Ellie? Does Suzette subtract the drink cost from the $45 that she owes Ellie for the room?

No. If Suzette subtracted it, then Suzette would pay $40 to Ellie *($45 - $5).*

Ellie would pay $50, which would be the total room charge of $90 minus the amount paid by Suzette *($40).*

That means Ellie would be paying $10 more than Suzette: Ellie paid $90 minus what Suzette paid $40, equals $50. Ellie would have to pay $10 more than Suzette *($50 - $40 = $10),* which is not correct if Ellie only owes Suzette $5 for the drink.

So how do we use math so that Ellie is only responsible for paying $5 more than Suzette for the room?

We calculate it by **first subtracting out the drink cost from the total bill** and then **splitting the room cost into two parts.** This means we first subtract and then we divide the number by 2.

$90 Room cost – Ellie paid

– $5 Drink Suzette paid for Ellie *(Suzette's payment toward room cost – by buying a drink for Ellie)*

$85 Revised room cost

Then we divide the revised room cost, $85, by 2. The forward slash is the division sign, /.

$85 / 2 *(divided by 2)* = $42.50 – Suzette's part of the room bill

So, to add it up, Suzette pays $42.50 toward the room cost, and Ellie pays $47.50 toward the room cost. Ellie pays $42.50 plus $5 for the drink to reimburse Suzette. $42.50 + $5 equals $47.50. Suzette will pay Ellie $42.50 to reimburse Ellie for Suzette's share of the room costs that Ellie paid up front, $90.

Double check your work to make sure you did the math correctly. Let's add the numbers to make sure each person paid their fair share:

Add $42.50 *(Suzette's portion of the bill)* and $47.50 *(Ellie's portion of the bill)* to equal the total room bill of $90. And now we double check to make sure Suzette is only paying $5 less than Ellie.

$47.50 *(Ellie's part)* minus $42.50 *(Suzette's part)* = $5 which is the amount Ellie owed Suzette for the drink.

To summarize, when dividing a bill between two people:

1) Subtract out the part that the person who paid less from the bill first.

2) Divide by the number of people paying to get the difference.

3) Add in the difference to the bill of the person who paid less, they will reimburse the person who paid more.

Split the Difference - Paying the Correct Amount Owed

You may have heard the term *"split the difference."* The way to square up the bill is to split the difference in payments made by each person.

Split the difference is used when people agree to split a bill. Each person pays different parts of the bill at different times and then wants to even up the payments. Some examples of this are expenses paid by two or more people for birthday parties, anniversary gifts, tickets, or trips. "

We will do the math for a story where Sally pays $150, and Amber pays $75 toward a birthday party and the ladies split the difference to even up their costs.

The Birthday Party: Splitting the Cost Between Two Friends

Sally and Amber decide to throw a party for Aurora, their friend, for her birthday. Sally bought food and drinks, and Amber bought party favors, napkins, plates, and the birthday cake. Sally and Amber decided on a total birthday budget of $225 or less.

Sally paid $150 for the food and drinks.

Amber paid $75 for the party favors, plates, napkins, and cake.

Note: to make it easier to do the math, write out the numbers below.

Friends each paid:

Sally	Amber
$150	$75

Most of the time, this unequal payment will happen with friends paying the bill. Someone *(like Sally)* pays for the more expensive items and the other friend *(like Amber)* pays for a less expensive item, and the amounts they paid are not equal. One has paid more than the other. How do we even up the amounts paid by the two ladies?

> **66** Plan your shopping trips by looking up the price before you go shopping. Decide with the person sharing the costs what the total budget will be, so there is no misunderstanding. **99**

First, let's split the difference now by subtracting Amber's bill from Sally's bill:

$150 Sally paid
– $75 Amber paid
$75 is the difference between what Sally paid and what Amber paid.

Second, let's split the difference between the ladies by dividing by 2 *($75/2=$37.50)*

The $75 difference, divided by 2, becomes $37.50, the split amount or reimbursement amount.

To even up the payments for both ladies, we will add the split amount, $37.50, to the lady's bill who paid less. Amber paid less *($75)*, so Amber owes Sally the split amount, $37.50.

Amber reimburses $37.50 to Sally in addition to what Amber already paid, $75, to equal $112.50.

Finally, let's do a quick sniff test to check to make sure the numbers are correct.

Amber

$75   Amber paid already

+$37.50   Amber pays Sally to reimburse her for paying more of the cost

$112.50   is the total cost that Amber would pay for her part of the birthday party

Sally

$150   Sally paid for food and drinks for the party

− $37.50   Amount she received from Amber as reimbursement *(subtract this, because Sally paid $150 and received Amber's payment)*

$112.50   is the total that Sally would pay for her part

Now as you can see, Sally paid $112.50, and Amber paid $112.50.

To summarize, to even up payments when one person pays more than the other person:

1) Subtract the smaller bill from the larger one.

2) Divide the resulting number by 2, which equals the split or reimbursement amount.

3) The person who paid less will pay the split or reimbursement amount to the person who paid more.

4) Always double-check your numbers to make sure both people pay the same amount.

After Amber reimburses Sally with $37.50, they can both say they split the cost of the party.

Key Money-Saving Tips

1) Practice manually adding and subtracting, which will help you memorize these operations and avoid relying on a calculator for everyday problems.

2) Create a shopping list before you shop at a grocery or other store and only buy items from the shopping list.

3) Compare prices at the grocery store for name brand groceries and the store brands to find the lowest price. Evaluate items on sale to determine if they are the best price.

4) Pay attention to the cost of items you buy and how they ring up at the check-out or payment screen if online.

5) When planning a trip or event, create a budget for the event, research the cost of the items in the list if you don't know the price, and purchase items on the list, sticking to the budget.

6) When dividing a bill between two people:

A. Subtract the amount the person paid who paid less from the amount the person who paid more to get the difference number.

B. Take the difference number and divide it by the number of people paying to get the split or reimbursement amount that the person who paid less owes the person who paid more.

C. The person who paid less owes this amount to the person who paid more.

7) If a person paid more for a group event and the group decided to split the expenses, determine how much the person who paid the most should be paid back *(reimbursed)*.

8) Review your receipts to ensure you are charged the correct amount *(sales price and number of items is correct)*. If it's not correct, notify the person who rang the purchase up and discuss the error.

Chapter 4

Multiply and Divide to Evaluate Deals

"When prosperity comes, do not use all of it."

-Confucius

Simple multiplication and division were taught in third grade in my school. Even though my parents insisted that I learn math and become an expert in it, I was not. I didn't understand multiplication tables. I was a right-brained kid; I loved art, painting, crafts, and creative arts. Why did I need to know math? I thought. Why should I have to excel in it as my parents wanted me to?

My sister was excellent in math naturally. But she was poor at art, whereas I excelled at it. She loved the fact that math does not change; it's always the same. Same formulas, same answers, tried and true, all the same. I, on the other hand, thought that things that were always the same were boring, and I loved to work in areas and projects that were constantly changing, or could change directions when a new idea was presented and tried.

Math is harder for some people because they never memorized their basic math multiplication tables or learned percents. As a result, many adults don't have the solid math foundation that is needed to help them make the best financial decisions.

Learning multiplication involves memorizing the multiplication tables or times tables. It's called the times tables, because when reading a column and row, we would say *six times seven,* hence the *"times"* tables. Multiplication tables are always the same; they don't change. Once a person memorizes the times tables, they will have the information for life. Memorizing the multiplication tables is a building block that will enable you to calculate more complex math problems. If you don't know your times tables, learning the higher math problems will be an uphill climb for you. The multiplication tables can be found in Appendix A.

> ★ **Math Hack Secret** ★
>
> Memorizing the multiplication tables is a building block that will enable you to calculate more complex math problems.

My dad insisted that I learn my multiplication *(times tables)* in third grade. So, he sat me down each evening after school and required that I memorize the times tables starting with the one times table, then twos, then threes, up to ten.

The one times tables looked simple: 1 X 1 = 1, 2 X 1 = 2. Pretty easy. If I saw 1 multiplied by 2, my answer was 2. Or 8 X 1, the answer would be 8. Then then we studied the 2 times tables. This was more difficult. I had memorized the addition tables, like 6 + 6 = 12, 5 + 5 = 10, 7 + 7 = 14. Because I had studied that 2 X 7 = 14, I would just think about adding up two sevens, or 7 + 7 = 14 and I could do a fairly good job of guessing the 2 times tables.

But when we had to memorize to 3- and 4-times tables and beyond, I couldn't guess anymore. I had to memorize the tables.

Some people say it was confusing to understand the times tables, where 6 X 4 is the same as adding 6 + 6 + 6 + 6. This would be four 6's, or 6 X 4.

My dad created a game for me. He challenged me to answer a multiplication problem by answering his times tables questions in two seconds. I found out it was hard to guess an answer to a multiplication question with a two-second window to respond. He required that I learn one row of multiplication times tables each night. *(e.g., 6 X 1 through 6 X 10)*. Every night he would challenge me with a question like, **"What is 6 times 7?"** Or he would switch it around and say, **"What is 7 times 6?"**

After studying the times tables for two or three weeks, I was able to answer all times tables question he would ask me within a second. This test helped me because in financial work, in life and in my career, I had to solve math problems quickly to answer a manager's question or to figure out cost savings for a project.

I recommend that you memorize the times tables like my dad asked me to do. Memorizing the times tables will help you quickly do math problems, so you can get the answer to your math question faster. In the back of the book, I recommend studying one row, *e.g.,* the 5's or 6's times tables for two days, then have someone test you. I recommend you start with the 2's times tables. See how quickly you can answer the times table questions, like **"What is 6 times 5?"** The faster you can answer the times tables question, the better you know it, and the faster you will learn and build on your math skills.

✎ **HELPFUL HINT:** Learn the 5 times tables especially well. Why? Because the U.S. currency and other currencies around the world have denominations in 5s. For example, in U.S. dollars: 5 cents, 10 cents, 25 cents, one, five, ten-, twenty-, fifty- and 100-dollar bills are all multiples of 5. The five times tables will help you count cash and help you know what you are owed or need to pay. We will look at how to count cash in Chapter 5.

Simple Multiplication and More Advanced Multiplication

Simple multiplication looks like this:

$$\begin{array}{r} 6 \\ \times\ 5 \\ \hline 30 \end{array}$$ or 6 X 5 = 30

Simple multiplication can be memorized in the times tables in Appendix A.

Double- and triple-digit multiplication looks like this:

$$\begin{array}{r} 45 \\ \times\ 9 \\ \hline \end{array}$$ or $$\begin{array}{r} 520 \\ \times\ 62 \\ \hline \end{array}$$

When would you see this math problem? We may need to solve it if we have a math problem like this:

Each automobile worker makes approximately forty-five car parts per day. Nine workers are working today in the factory. How many car parts can we plan for them to make today?

How do we solve it manually, which means writing it out and showing our work? Why do we solve it manually rather than using a calculator? Because it will help you practice math problems, so you become better at multiplication. Since multiplication and decimals are used daily, practicing these calculations manually will help you improve your mental math skills, allowing you to quickly solve problems without needing a calculator.

Rows and Columns

As a refresher, to solve a multiplication or division problem, you will use rows and columns to keep track of the numbers that are added or subtracted. Rows are the numbers across from left to right, and columns show the numbers that are on the top and bottom. For example, the math problem below has rows and columns.

```
  45 - Row 1
X 9 - Row 2
───
  45
X 9
───
 ↑↑ - These arrows show the columns
```

How to Solve Double-Digit Multiplication Problems

As with all multiplication problems, we start by multiplying the rightmost column and then moving left. The number on the bottom row, far right number, is 9. Multiply the 9 with the top right number on the top row, which is 5. *(9 X 5 = 45.)* We can only place one number, the 5 so we have to carry the 4 to the next column at the top. Multiply the bottom row number with the second number on the top to the left, which is 4. *(9 X 4 = 36.)*

```
  4
  45
X 9 - 9 X 5, then 9 X 4
───
  ↑
```

```
  4 ← 4 is carried to the next column
  45
X 9
───
  5 ← Place the 5 here
```

Next, we multiply the 9 X 4 and get 36.

Add the 36 to the number on top that carried over, which is 4. 36 + 4 = 40.

Place the 40 next to the 5 and the resulting number is 405.

$$
\begin{array}{r}
{}^{4} \\
45 \\
\times\ \ 9 \\
\hline
405
\end{array}
$$

45 X 9 = 405. We can estimate that the nine workers will make a total of 405 car parts in a day.

Let's try a two-digit multiplication problem that is a word problem.

Math Problem: We hired additional workers, so now we have twenty-five workers working in the automobile plant.

Each worker makes forty-five parts per day on average.

How many parts can we expect to be completed in one day using 25 workers?

$$
\begin{array}{l}
25\ \ \text{workers} \\
\underline{\times\,45}\ \ \text{parts per day}
\end{array}
$$

Each number on the bottom, the 4 and the 5, are multiplied by the two numbers on the top, the 2 and the 5.

We still carry numbers to the next column that are greater than 9. But now we have two rows of answers to add.

⚠ **TRICK:** Count the numbers in the bottom row. In this problem, there are two numbers, 4 and 5. That means that your math problem will have two rows of numbers, which you will add once you write them in the rows.

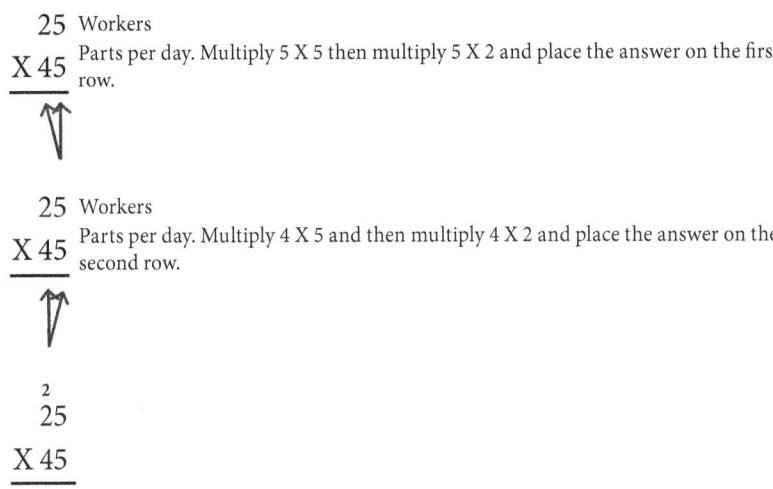

25 Workers
X 45 Parts per day. Multiply 5 X 5 then multiply 5 X 2 and place the answer on the first row.

25 Workers
X 45 Parts per day. Multiply 4 X 5 and then multiply 4 X 2 and place the answer on the second row.

2
25
X 45

5   5 X 5 = 25, put the 5 under the right column, and carry the 2 to the next column.

Multiply the 5 with the next number to the left, the 2. 5 X 2 = 10. Add the carried number 2 to 10 to equal 12.

$$\begin{array}{r} \overset{2}{2}5 \\ \times\ 45 \\ \hline 125 \end{array}$$

We are finished with multiplying 5 in the first column to the top row, numbers 2 and 5. The answer, 125, is written in the first row. Let's multiply the 4 in the second column with the numbers above it.

$$\begin{array}{r} 25 \\ \times\ 45 \\ \hline 125 \end{array}$$

We will now multiply the 4, with the 5 and 2 above it. We start writing the answers in a second row starting under the 4. It's important to line up the rows of numbers so you will get the correct answer.

²
25
X 45
___
125
0 → 4 X 5 = 20, place the zero under the 4 column and carry the 2 to the next column to the left above the 2 on the 25 number.

²
25
X 45
___
125
100 → Multiply the 4 X 2 = 8 and add 2 *(which is carried over)* to the answer which is 10. Put the 10 next to the 0 for the second row

To get the answer, we need to add the two rows below the math problem, 125 and the 100, The 100 has a silent zero on the end, so we see 100 as adding like it is 1,000.

125
100
___
1125

1,125 parts per day can be made by workers if the plant had 25 workers working per day.

A three-digit number multiplied with another three-digit number is the same, except we now have three rows of answers to add.

568
X 433
___

The first row looks like this when multiplied.

2 2
568
X 433
____
1704 ← Row 1

3 X 8 = 24; carry the 2 to the next column. 3 X 6 = 18 and add the 2 from the carry = 20. Write the zero and carry the 2 to the next column.

3 X 5 = 15 and add the 2 that carried = 17.

The first row then is 1704.

Let's multiply the second row using the 3 in the second column *(same calculation as row 1)*:

<pre>
    2 2
   568
 X 433
  1704 ← Row 1
  1704 ← Row 2
</pre>

3 X 8 = 24, write the 4 and carry the 2. 3 X 6 = 18 and add the carried 2 = 20, write in the 0 and carry the 2. 3 X 5 = 15 and add the 2 to be 17. Write in the 17. You are finished with row 2.

Let's calculate row 3 now.

4 X 8 = 32, write the 2 and carry the 3. 4 X 6 = 24 plus the 3 = 27. Write the 7 and carry the 2. 4 X 5 = 20. Add the 2 that was carried to the next column, which adds up to be 22. Write the 22. You are finished with row 3.

<pre>
    2 3
   568
 X 433
  1704 ← Row 1
  1704 ← Row 2
 2272   ← Row 3
</pre>

Now we can add the rows because we lined up the columns by putting the numbers in the rows in the correct columns. Lining up the numbers in the correct column is important, so we can find the correct answer.

```
      568
   X 433
   ─────
     1704
     1704|
     2272||
   ╨╨╨╨╨╨
   245944
```

Add the numbers for each column and place the number under the column:

```
      568
   X 433
   ─────
     1704
     1704
   +2272
   ─────
   245944
```

568 X 433 = 245,944

On a math calculator, we would enter 568, then tap the multiplication symbol *(X)*, then enter 433, and then tap the equals sign, and the answer will appear 245,944.

Story Word Problem to Solve: Visit to the Pharmacy – Deal or No Deal?

You visit your favorite pharmacy and want to buy some multi-vitamins for yourself and your family.

The sign on the shelf says, *"Buy one, get one for 50% off."*

Is it a deal or not? Is it worth buying or passing on the vitamin sale? Is it really a sale? Let's find out.

The price on the sign for the sale vitamins is $11.99. Let's call it Vitamin X.

Let's do the math to figure out how much each bottle of vitamins would cost if we bought two bottles of the vitamins on sale, calculating both the total price, and the price per bottle.

$11.99 for one bottle of vitamins

Plus 50% of $11.99 for the second bottle of vitamins

To do the math, we need to find the price of a bottle of vitamins at 50% off, which is half price. Then we can add that price to the full price of the second bottle of vitamins to equal our total cost.

To find the discounted vitamin cost, we must convert the percent, 50%, to a decimal which is .50. Remember to move over the decimal point two places from the right to left of the percent sign. 50% = .50.

Now we can multiply .50 times the price *($11.99)* of the vitamins.

$$\begin{array}{r} \$11.99 \text{ Price of first bottle} \\ \underline{X \quad .50 \text{ is 50\% off}} \\ \$5.99 \text{ price of the second bottle} \end{array}$$

So, the price of the second bottle rounded up to the nearest dollar is $6.

One bottle of vitamins is $11.99, and the second bottle of vitamins is $6.

The deal is to buy two bottles of vitamins, so let's add the one to the other.

$11.99 + $6 = $17.99

$17.99 is the price for two bottles of vitamins. But what is the price for **each** bottle if we bought two?

We need to know the average price, because we want to compare the price per bottle of the sale vitamins to the regular price of one bottle of vitamins sitting on the shelf next to the sale vitamins.

Let's take the total $17.99 and divide by 2 to get the price of each bottle of vitamins.

$17.99 ÷ 2 = $8.995 which rounded up is $9. So, the 50% off deal will cost you $9 per bottle of vitamins.

When you have this number *($9)*, you can compare it to other vitamins that are not on sale but could be a better deal than the sale vitamins.

On the shelf next to the sale vitamins *(Vitamin X)* are another brand of vitamins called Vitamin Y. This bottle contains vitamins that are just as potent, have the same ingredients, and the same number of pills in the bottle. This bottle is priced at $8.

Which vitamins are a better deal? Vitamin X is on sale: buy one at $11.99 and get 50% off the second bottle, or the second deal, buy a single bottle of Vitamin Y for $8?

To determine which vitamins are a better deal, we need to look at the price per bottle.

Vitamin X – Buy one, get one at 50% off. Our price per bottle is $9, which we calculated above.

Vitamin Y – Buy a bottle of vitamins for $8. We don't have to buy 2 bottles to get this deal.

What vitamins would you buy? $9 per bottle or $8 per bottle?

If the vitamins are the same for Vitamin X as Vitamin Y, then why not save $1 and buy the $8 bottle of Vitamin Y?

A Division Problem: We Won the Lottery!

Being able to divide to solve problems is just as important as being able to multiply. Both can be done using a calculator, but I recommend practicing doing the math by hand because it will sharpen your skills. Let's figure out how ten men split a winning lottery ticket. This story uses division to get the answer.

Ten men put in money for a group of tickets for a chance to win the lottery, and one ticket won them $50,000. They decided previously that each man would receive an equal share of the money. How much does each man get?

$50,000 is split by ten men. The math problem is set up like this: $50,000 / 10 = X$

So, we need to do the math: 50,000 divided by 10 to find the X, or the amount each man wins.

Below we will calculate a division problem manually.

$$10\overline{)50000}$$ (10 into 50,000 equals the dollars that are paid to each man)

How do we solve this problem? The divisor is 10 and the dividend is 50,000. The dividend is the number that is being divided. The quotient *(the answer)* will be the number placed above the horizontal line.

First, look for the first group of numbers that 10 can divide into. Can 10 divide into 5? No, let's try 10 into 50? Yes. 50 divided by 10 is 5.

So, the first number is 5. Write it above the line above the zero on the 50. Lining up the numbers in a division problem is very important.

$$\begin{array}{r} 5 \\ 10\overline{)50000} \end{array}$$

Now write the 50 *(5X10)* in row 1 under the first two digits of the number 500 *(below the line in row 1)*.

$$\begin{array}{r} 5 \\ 10\overline{)50000} \\ 50 \end{array}$$ ← put 50 here in row 1

How do you know you did it right? Double check it by multiplying the 5 from above the line by the 10 to the left, and the resulting number should be 50 written below the line.

Now subtract the 50 from 50 to get zero. Write the zero in the second column, under the zero.

Drop down the next number from the top, which is zero. To do this division problem, the number right below the line, which is zero is dropped down to the next row, which is row 2.

$$
\begin{array}{r}
5 \\
10\overline{)50000} \\
50\Big\downarrow \\
00 \leftarrow \text{row 2}
\end{array}
$$

Next ask: 10 divided into zero is? Zero. If you have nothing, you get nothing *(zero)*.

Place the zero to the right of the 5.

$$
\begin{array}{r}
50 \\
10\overline{)50000} \\
50 \\
00 \leftarrow \text{row 2}
\end{array}
$$

There are only zeros now to drop down from the right side, 10 into zero is zero, do this twice. So, the answer is the number above the line, which is $5,000. $50,000 divided by 10 is $5,000.

$$
\begin{array}{r}
5000 \leftarrow \text{your answer is 5000} \\
10\overline{)50000} \\
50 \\
00 \leftarrow \text{row 2} \\
00 \leftarrow \text{row 3}
\end{array}
$$

Double check your work: make sure 10 X 5000 = 50,000.

The answer is that each man will get $5,000 in lottery money.

Another way to do this math is to use the calculator: Enter 50,000, press the key ÷ *(divided by sign)*, and then enter the number 10 *(the number dividing into the 50,000)* and press the = sign.

Football Ticket Purchase: Deal or No Deal

Let's look at an opportunity that Adam has to buy football tickets and do the math to make sure he is paying a fair price for the tickets.

Football Season Tickets: How Much Should Adam Pay?

A football season ticket holder has decided to sell her tickets for the whole season because she will be out of the country during that entire time period.

She offers the tickets to Adam to buy. The tickets are for ten home games. She has two tickets to sell for each game. She is offering to sell the tickets for $2,000 for all ten games.

Adam will need to determine how many tickets he will be buying as well as the cost per ticket. Knowing these details will help him decide if the sales price is a good enough price.

Here is the information to figure out how many tickets are available to buy.

    10 home games
    2 tickets to each game
    10 X 2 = 20 tickets being sold by the seller

Now let's figure out the price per ticket.

Simply take the price for all the tickets, $2,000 and divide it by the number of tickets *(20)* to get the price per ticket of $100.

First, does the price per ticket seem fair? $100 per seat per game? How do we check if it is a good deal? One way is to access the Internet and find ticket-selling websites and look up the price for similar seats to determine the average price per seat. If the website sells similar seats for $80 per seat, does $100 per seat seem reasonable?

That is a choice Adam will have to consider.

If Adam bought the $80 seats instead and purchased two seats per game for the 10 home season games, how much would he spend on tickets *(not including fees)*?

> $80 *(per ticket)* X 2 seats X 10 home games
> $80 X 2 X 10 = $1,600
> $1,600 is the cost if he bought tickets from a website ticket seller.

To calculate the amount he would pay for tickets from the friend, we do the math:

> $100 *(per ticket)* X 2 seats X 10 home games
> $100 X 2 X 10 = $2,000
> $2,000 is the cost if Adam bought his friend's tickets.

Double check your numbers and do a sniff test to ensure accuracy.

$1,600 can be paid for 20 tickets. This price is less than the friend's $2,000 ticket price deal.

It may appear that the $1,600 deal is better than the $2,000 deal for tickets. However, Adam should also look at the location of the seats in the stadium, which seats have a better view of the game, and any fees he would have to pay from buying them online. Some online sellers may a charge ten or twenty percent fee in addition to the ticket price. Double check the fees charged by online ticket sellers before deciding to buy tickets online.

Doing the math gives you options, so you can make smart choices.

Key Money-Saving Tips

1) Learning the multiplication tables makes multiplication problems much easier. Memorize the multiplication tables and then ask someone to test you on each one. Start with the 2's and work your way up to the 10's times tables.

2) When multiplying, multiply the numbers from the right to the left side of the problem, always starting with the number on the bottom-right side of the equation.

3) For division problems, divide from the left to the right side of the equation.

4) Use math to determine the individual price of items, like tickets, which may be sold in large quantities.

5) Record the savings in your Money Keeping Journal.

Chapter 5

Learn to Count Back Cash

"You may delay, but time will not."

–Benjamin Franklin

You may have heard the term, ***"Cash is King."*** What does this mean? It means that people who have cash available to spend or invest are in a better position to negotiate prices on various things.

I think everyone should have cash in their wallet or purse to make daily purchases. You don't need to have a substantial amount of money but enough to pay for your daily expenses. If you only have a day's cash on hand, you may spend less because you can see the dollars leaving your hands as you hand the clerk payment for a purchase. Actually seeing the money you're spending can be more impactful than using a debit or credit card.

Debit and credit cards are easy to use for purchases. But sometimes stores and restaurants will charge you a convenience fee for using a credit card. I have experienced the stores charging a 3% fee on top of the total purchase amount. Having cash handy will help you eliminate convenience fees, particularly on a higher priced purchase. Cash purchases do not incur convenience fees.

When I was a teenager, I worked part-time at the fast-food chain, Wendy's. All cash registers at the time did not display the change that was owed to the customer. The cash register only displayed the total bill the customer owed. So, we had to count back change to give the customer the correct amount of money. Either we learned to count back change, or we had to pull out the calculator and subtract the total bill from the dollar bills that the customer gave us. Most cash registers today have changed and will display the change to give to the customer.

66 Why is counting cash important? It matters to customers who deserve to get back the cash and change they deserve. 99

Why is counting cash important? It matters to customers who deserve to get back the cash and change they deserve.

Retail clerks or others who give you change should be counting it back to you. What does this mean? Let's give an example: If you buy a hamburger or veggie burger for $5, you give Allison, the clerk, a $20 bill. She should count back your change from the price of the burger up to the dollar amount you gave her. She starts counting from the price of the hamburger, five dollars, and then gives you a $5 dollar bill, says *"$10"* and gives you a $10 bill, and says *"$20 dollars."* If the clerks are not counting back change to you, they may not have been taught how to do this.

For example, if the bill was $8.91 and the customer gave you a $20 bill, how do you give the person the correct change? You may have a cash register that shows you the amount of change to give back. But just giving back change without counting it back doesn't help you master giving back change or knowing that you received the correct change from your purchase.

To count back change, you count from $8.91 up to the $20 bill they gave you. Like the situation just described, there is a trick to doing this.

Here is how it works:

We start with the total bill and count up to the amount the person gives the clerk, using coins first, then dollars. In U.S. currency, we count up using pennies, nickels, dimes, quarters, one-dollar bills, five-dollar bills, ten-dollar bills, twenty-dollar bills and up.

Use each currency to *"bump up"* to get to the next currency. Counting up from $8.91 to $20 looks like this:

We first start with the total cost of the purchase: $8.91.

The counting process is to count up from pennies through the currency like this:

One cent to increase to the next currency *(nickels)* would be four cents to five cents. Start at one cent, add four more cents. This brings the number to $8.95.

Now we can start adding nickels, dimes, and quarters to count up from $8.95 to $9. This would add be one nickel or five cents.

Now we need to find the change to count up from $9 to $10.

From $9 to $10, we add a one-dollar bill.

Then to find the change to count up from $10 to $20, we add a ten-dollar bill or two five-dollar bills.

How much change did we just make?

In your hand, you have four pennies, one nickel, one dollar, and one ten-dollar bill.

Add it up: .04 + .05 + $1 + $10 = $11.09

Rather than pulling out a calculator to do this math, you can count up and get the same number. It's a faster way to count change.

In summary, we start with $8.91, and add nine cents, a dollar, and ten dollars, which equals $11.09 change from the twenty dollars, which is what the customer gave the clerk.

Making change from $8.91 with a $20 payment.

> $0.91 – $1.00 is 9 cents
> $9 to $10 *(the next currency)* = $1
> $10 to $20 = $10

The change in your hand should be the difference between the $20 bill you received and the $8.91 that is the amount owed. In your hand will be four pennies, a nickel, a one-dollar bill, and a 10-dollar bill totaling $11.09. Count back the change to a customer by counting up from $8.91 to $20.

> From $8.91, say **"nine"** *(and give them the four pennies and one nickel)*
> Say **"ten"** *(give them the $1)* and
> Say **"twenty"** and give them the $10 bill.

People will really appreciate it when you count back the change to them. It shows that they are receiving the correct change.

Also, it will save you some aggravation if the customer receives the change and says, ***"No, I gave you a 50-dollar bill for the purchase."*** If you are receiving cash from someone and have to make change, make sure you keep the currency the person gave you on the register drawer so there is no dispute. You can show the customer the bills you were given.

When you give change back, line up the fronts faces of the dollar bills to count back to the customer. When the faces of the dollar bills are upside down or the back of the dollar bill is facing up, it's hard to see what denomination of dollars you are getting back.

Counting back change is also important for you if you are the one buying the hamburger.

How many times does the clerk hand you a bunch of dollar bills and change and say, *"Here you go. Here's your change!"*

How do you know you received the right amount of change? You know because you can count back the change they gave you to yourself to make sure you received the correct change. Don't be ripped off; count your change back when you receive it.

An additional question – let's say your bill is $30.50 and you give the clerk $40.50. How much does the clerk owe you in change? Quick math in your head is $40.50 minus $30.50 = $10.

Why give the clerk $40.50? Because the change back will result in fewer bills and change in your pocket to carry around. If you gave the clerk $40, the change would be $9.50. This change is one five-dollar bill, four one-dollar bills, and fifty cents. But if you gave the clerk $40.50, then your change would be $10, which is one bill, and a lot easier to carry around!

Counting Back Helps You Catch Errors

Watch your change so a clerk doesn't make a mistake with your money and leave you short. Once I gave a clerk a $100 bill, and my total was $8.25. She gave me 75 cents, a one-dollar bill, one 10-dollar bill, and three 20-dollar bills.

If I wasn't counting back the cash she gave me, I would have missed that she did not give me one $20 bill back that I was owed.

Below is the change that I should have received, by counting up from $8.25 to $100:

$8.25 → $9   75 cents
$9   → $10   1 dollar
$10   → $20   10-dollar bill
$20   → $100 4 20-dollar bills

The total I should have received was $91.75.

She gave me change for $80, as I counted the change back to myself:

$8.25 → $9   75 cents
$9   → $10   1 dollar
$10   → $20   10-dollar bill
$20   → $100 3 20-dollar bills

She gave me change totaling $71.75.

I asked her to check the $100 bill I gave her, and I showed her the change she gave me. She quickly realized her error and gave me the other $20 that I was owed.

This could happen to you if you are not counting back your change after you receive it from a clerk. Be smart with your money; always count back change to yourself to make sure it's the right amount. Also count back change you give to others.

Key Money-Saving Tips

1) Always check the cash you receive back from a purchase to ensure you receive the correct change.

2) Count back change to someone if you work at a cash register or if you are paying someone back. It shows you know your numbers. Even if most cash registers tell the clerk and customer how much change the customer should receive, counting back can help you catch errors. This skill is also important at venues like farmers markets where vendors might not use a cash register.

3) Use change in your pocket to make small purchases, enjoy the purchase, and get rid of coins as well.

4) Keep track of your savings by recording it in your Money Keeping Journal.

Chapter 6

Calculate Sales Tax and Split Checks Fairly

"Without continual growth and process, such words as improvement, achievement, and success have no meaning."

-Benjamin Franklin

In earlier chapters, we did not calculate sales tax on purchases. Not adding sales tax made the math problems easier to understand and to solve. However, since there is tax added to many items you buy, it's worth understanding how much tax you're paying.

To figure out how to split a restaurant check, you first need to know how to calculate sales tax on an order. Most states add sales tax to restaurant bills as well as other purchases.

Let's use an example of calculating sales tax on a customer's plumbing work order.

For example, Aaron provides plumbing services and products for customers. He goes to people's homes and assesses how many hours it will take him to perform the work and what plumbing parts he will use. The customer accepts his price estimate, and Aaron works on the job and finishes the work.

At the end of the job, he writes an invoice so the customer can pay his company for the work he completed. The customer pulls out the credit card to pay for the work. How does Aaron calculate sales tax on the parts and add labor to the bill? How does Aaron know if he is charging the correct amount?

Let's look at Aaron's invoice and help him calculate sales tax on the order:

Aaron's Plumbing Bill
Plumbing Supplies: $50 plus sales tax
Aaron's Labor: $200 for two hours. His state does not charge sales tax on his labor.
Total: $250

What is the sales tax on the order? Only the $50 in supplies is subject to sales tax. Let's say sales tax is 8.375%.

How much sales tax does Aaron charge to the invoice?

$50 is sales taxable – plumbing parts.
8.375% is the sales tax rate for his state.

We know that 8.375% is actually .08375 in decimal form, which we convert from a percent to a decimal. So, we can do the math. Now let's multiply it out:

$50 X .08375 = $4.1875

We round it up to $4.19 in sales tax.

Now let's add it all up:

Supplies:	$50
Labor:	$200
Sales tax:	$4.19
Total:	$254.19

Aaron will write the invoice with a breakout of the three charges as shown above, and the total amount due. Then he can collect the total amount from the customer.

If you don't know how to calculate sales tax, and you are out in the field or have no one to ask, you will not be able to finish the invoice for the customer. If you run a business or are a vendor, you should learn how to calculate sales tax and know the sales tax rate for the city or county where the job is located.

Here is another example. Remember the woman who wants to buy a shirt? She has $50 in her pocket. The shirt on is sale for 20% off the regular price which is $50. How much will the shirt cost if you include sales tax?

Remember, the shirt is discounted 20%.

So, 20% of $50 is $10 *(.20 X $50 = $10)*
New sales price is $50 - $10 *(discount at 20% off)* = $40
Sales tax on $40 is $40 X .08375 = $3.35

Total cost of the shirt is $40 plus sales tax, $3.35 = $43.35

She has $50. Can she buy the shirt with the cash she has on hand?

Yes, and the change she will receive back is $6.65.

Let's count back the change she received to double check it. She hands the clerk $50 in cash. The bill is $43.25. Let's count up from $43.25 to $50 to determine the change received.

$43.35 → $44   65 cents *(5 cents + 1 dime + 2 quarters)*
$44   → $45   1 dollar
$45   → $50   5 dollars

Add it up to $6.65. $0.65 + $1 + $5 = $6.65. Her change should be $6.65.

Going Out to Dinner and Splitting the Bill?

You probably have had this experience: You and two friends go to a restaurant for dinner. When the bill comes, everyone must figure out how much they should pay, calculate sales tax if applicable, and then calculate a tip for the waiter.

Sometimes friends just add on the tip and split the bill by the number of people. But if someone ordered an alcoholic drink, appetizer, or dessert, and the others did not, splitting the bill evenly could be unfair to those who ordered less expensive items.

While some people may be comfortable splitting the bill regardless of whether one individual ordered a more expensive item, generally people prefer to split the bill based on what they ordered.

If you are the person who ordered more, it's a good idea to say that you will pay more of the total bill because you ordered more expensive items than the rest of the dinner group. If the rest of the diners say it doesn't matter and they want to split the bill evenly, then you can do so.

However, if they don't insist on splitting the bill evenly, then you must know how to accurately calculate what you owe. You don't want to be the person who shortchanges others because you didn't pay your fair share. If that happens, then the other people must pay more money on the bill to cover your part, and you become *"persona non-invited"* to the next dining event!

When you hear, *"Ah, we only have enough to cover the bill, and part of the tip,"* then you know the restaurant bill is underpaid because someone did not calculate their tip correctly or forgot to add sales tax to their meal cost.

Some people forget to add the sales tax to their part of the bill and just pay the cost of the food, drink and tip. Others don't know how to calculate a tip.

Story of Three Friends Who Went Out to Dinner Together

Sherry, Fred, and Mina decide to dine out one evening. The restaurant has a great *"special"* on a rack of lamb. Fred orders the special without asking about the price, which is not on the menu. Sherry orders her usual choice, and Mina is on a fat trimming diet and a budget diet, too. She orders smaller portions and water to fit within her budget. They have a great meal and good conversation.

> ### ★ Math Hack Secret ★
>
> My experience with dinner specials is that if the server offers a special and it's not on the menu or posted anywhere in the restaurant, the special may have an especially high price, which often is 20 – 30% more expensive than the other dinner options on the menu. I suggest you ask what the price is for the dinner special if the waiter does not tell you when describing the special. If the price works for you, then order the dinner if you want. If the price of the special doesn't work, then you just saved 20 – 30% on the meal.

The waiter drops off the bill after the three friends finish their meal. It looks like this.

Beef Stroganoff: $20
Rack of lamb: $40
Beer *(3)*: $30
Cabernet wine: $10
Side salad: $10
Subtotal: $110

Tax *(9%)*: $9.90
Total: $119.90

Everyone takes turns looking at the bill. Mina scratches her head and doesn't know what she owes. Fred doesn't know that the tip should not be calculated on the sales tax portion of the bill. Sherry hates math because she doesn't understand how to split a bill and turns the bill over to Fred.

Fred says, ***"Why don't we just split the bill?"*** Mina protests, politely telling him that she can't afford to pay for his drinking habit and fine taste in cuisine. Fred is busted and realizes he can't convince others to pay his part of the bill, or he hates math and has no clue what he owes. Either way, let's help these friends determine what portion of the bill they need to pay.

The bill should be divided this way:

Sherry
Beef Stroganoff: $20
Cabernet wine: $10
Total: $30
Fred
Rack of lamb: $40
3 beers: $30
Total: $70
Mina
Side salad: $10
Glass of ice water: *(free)*
Total: $10

For the state where they're dining, the sales tax is 9% on food and drink. They will have to add the sales tax to their meal costs. Each state and county may have a different sales tax rate for food and drink purchases. Some states don't charge sales tax on restaurant meals, although most do. The group decides to pay a 20% tip to the waiter.

You can tip the waiter or waitress any amount you choose, based on the quality of the service. If the service was lacking, the waiter ignored you, brought out cold food, was arrogant or irate, or did not make you feel valued as a customer, then tip what you feel is the right amount for the service provided.

First, save some money by doing this: Don't pay tips on the sales tax portion of the bill.

You are not tipping on the sales tax you owe on the bill. If you do tip on tax, then you are spending more money than needed. Some people pay tips on the tax because they don't understand how tipping works. Others add it on because they don't care and want to tip the food server more.

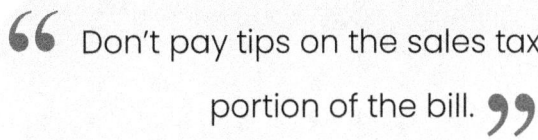

“ Don't pay tips on the sales tax portion of the bill. ”

If you are diligent with your money and want to pay only what you owe and a tip, then save money and don't pay a tip on the sales tax portion. Saving money here will add up. Enter the amount saved by not tipping on tax into your Money Keeping Journal.

Always take the time to review the itemized bill presented to the table. Sometimes when credit cards are presented to the food server, the server runs the credit cards and returns with the credit card bills, which only have the total on each bill, and no detailed items ordered. Make sure you can have the detailed bill handy. Then when you write in the tip and total and sign your name, you are paying tip on the sub-total and not the total bill which may include sales tax.

Sherry's bill plus tip
$30 bill
Tip at 20% of $30 is $6 tip.
So, convert 20% to .20 and multiply by $30.
.20 X $30 = $6

★ Math Hack Secret ★

An easy way to quickly figure out what a 20% tip would be is to multiply 10 percent by the subtotal of the bill before tax and then double it. For example, 10% of a $30 bill = $3. Double $3 and you get a $6 tip, which is a 20% tip. This is important so you can save time by calculating the tip quickly without having to pull out the phone calculator to do the math.

Sherry's bill with tip: $30 food/drink bill + $6 tip = $36 total
Sales tax of 9% on Sherry's bill of $30 = 9% of $30
.09 X $30 = $2.70
$2.70 = sales tax

⚠ **TRICK:** An easy way to calculate sales tax in the above example is to multiply 30 X 9 = 270. Then move decimal point to the left 2 places, which equals $2.70.

Total bill for Sherry is $2.70 tax + $30 food + $6 tip = $38.70

What is Mina's bill?

Her bill is easier. She pays $10 for the salad, plus tax and tip.

Since we don't pay tip on tax, her tip amount would be $2 *(20% of $10 meal)*
(.20 X 10 = $2)

What is her tax amount? For the state they live in, the tax is 9%.

So, 9% of $10 food bill is: .09 X $10 = $0.90 or ninety cents in tax.

Let's add up her total bill: $0.90 tax + $2 tip + $10 food bill = $12.90.

Fred's bill $70 owed before tax and tip.

Tax on the bill is $70 X .09 = $6.30 *(Quick multiplication is 7 X 9 = 63.)*

Tip on $70 at 20% is .20 X $70 = $14 *(visually 7 X 2 = 14)*

Add Fred's bill plus tax and tip: $70 + $14 + $6.30 = $90.30.

When all the money is combined to pay the total bill, and everyone pays the sales tax on their part of the bill, plus the agreed upon tip of 20 percent, the payment for each person looks like this:

Mina - $12.90
Sherry - $38.70
Fred - $90.30
          ————
          $141.90

After everyone puts their money on the table or provides a credit card to pay, the total bill paid should be about $141. Some people round the bill up or down, so this is an estimate.

Some people use the subtotal of their meal and add 25% to include the tip and tax. It may work in some states, but for other states that have a 10 or 11% sales tax rate, it won't work well there. Let's look at the reason why using a 10% sales tax rate below:

   20% tip
+ 10% sales tax rate
————
   30% total — which is more than the 25% some dinner groups pay, so the waiter receives less tip *(25% - 9% (sales tax)) = 16%* tip) for the waiter, which is less than the party intended to tip the waiter at 20%.

Double Check Your Bill for Accuracy

When you receive the bill for the meal, double check the items on the bill for accuracy. Sometimes, items will be added to the bill that you did not order. The waiter may have made a mistake when adding the items to the bill. If you see any items that you or your fellow diners didn't order, let your waiter know about the error and ask for a revised bill that has the correct total.

Tipping

A tip is a small gratuity paid to servers for their service. In the United States, tipping on food service is to reward servers who provide good service. Some fast-food restaurants and drive through coffee shops ask for tips, too. It's up to you to decide which server should be tipped.

If the food server or other server does not provide good or great service, you can choose to tip the individual a smaller amount or nothing. I personally believe that if the service is so lousy, and you don't want to tip the person at all, it would be a good idea to tell the individual that the service was substandard, and that is why you aren't leaving a tip or are leaving a smaller tip. If you don't want to speak to the server, then leave spare change *(quarters, dimes, nickels, etc.)* on the table before you leave, which should indicate that you feel you received poor or non-existent service.

Look for a Gratuity Charge (Tip) Included in the Bill

If you have a larger party, such as six or more people, some restaurants will charge 18% or 20% tip to the entire bill and call it gratuity. If you have a party of six or more, check to see if a gratuity was added to the total bill. If the tip is added in, you don't have to add any extra tip, unless you want to reward the server and pay an additional tip.

If you are curious whether a charge on the bill called a service charge or gratuity is actually a built-in tip for the server, ask your server for clarification. Some restaurants charge a service charge or gratuity and pass the tip along to the server. Other restaurants don't pass the service charge or gratuity along to the server.

> ### ★ Math Hack Secret ★
>
> Always look to see whether a gratuity has been added to your bill before you add one. Even casual dining restaurants and coffee shops have started to include gratuities on bills.

Look at your bill in other venues as well, such as when ordering drinks on a cruise ship, pre-paid group activities, and other events where someone is providing a service to you. Always check your bill for an added gratuity before you pay the bill. Then you can determine if you want to add additional gratuity.

Even if you ask for separate dinner checks for each person or couple in a large party setting *(six or more people)*, the food server could still add a gratuity to everyone's separate bill, because you were part of a larger party. Look for the automatic gratuity on your bill for a larger group. You don't want to double pay a tip because you didn't review the bill before you paid it.

Some people I dine with always ask for separate checks. I'm curious to know if:

1) They don't know how to figure out what they owe on a group bill, or

2) They hate math, or

3) They plan on tipping less than the rest and don't want any-one to know.

Samuel and the Dining Group

We had a friend named Samuel. He would always want to dine at exclusive *(expensive)* restaurants. Eight of us would dine together. I lost count on the number of drinks Samuel consumed. He started out with multiple dirty martinis and then ordered a couple of bottles of wine and poured each person one glass and then consumed the rest all by himself.

When the bill came to the table after the meal, the math hacks went to work figuring out what they owed on the bill, added a tip, then calculated tax. The tipsy ones weren't thinking at all and just wanted to split the bill. However, some of the diners did not drink alcohol and only had iced tea or water. Most of us had cash to put in because it's easier than giving the waiter multiple credit cards.

Samuel would wait until all the cash was put on the table. Then he would scoop up the cash and put down a credit card to pay the bill. Since the group was generous with the tips they left, he would add cash only up to what the bill was, skimp on the tip, and pocket the differ-ence, which made his meal cost about half of what it should have been.

A guy named Olin did not drink; he only had a soda and food. Olin said he didn't drink and wanted to pay his part of the food bill. Samuel didn't take Olin's lower priced meal into consideration. The rest of us agreed with Olin that, since he didn't drink wine with the rest of the group, he should pay less. Samuel relented and the math hacks calculated the amount that Olin owed. If you behave like Samuel and do not respect the people who order less and should therefore pay less of the bill, others may not want to hang out with you. This is another reason it's good to understand math!

Note, if you are like Skinny Mina and don't buy expensive meals in a group setting, I advise that you bring cash for the meal, and pay the group with cash, which includes your food, tax, and tip.

Then if multiple people pull out credit cards to pay, they can decide among themselves who owes what for the rest of the meal.

Key Money-Saving Tips

1) Always add your part of a bill and pay the tip on the subtotal part of the bill, not the total bill. The tip should be paid on the food and drink, not on the sales tax.

2) Always check the dining bill to see if a tip was automatically added. If so, the tip has been paid already. You don't have to add a tip unless you want to pay an additional tip. It's your choice.

3) Always look out for those who order less on a group dining bill. Ask them what they think they owe because their part of the food or drink was less. They will appreciate you.

4) Don't just split the bill at a restaurant or on a trip. Review all charges on the bill to make sure that splitting the bill makes sense.

5) Double check your bill when you receive it from the waiter. Check every item to ensure you are not charged for food or drink that you did not order.

6) Write down your savings from better-priced meals, and money you saved by not paying tips on tax in your Money Keeping Journal.

Chapter 7

Picking the Best Deal on Credit Cards and Bank Accounts

"If you buy things you do not need, soon
you will have to sell things you need."

–Warren Buffett

A man named Mike goes into a bank and tells the bank teller he wants to open a credit card. Sheila, the bank teller, asks him what type of card he wants. Mike likes the color red, so he asks about the red card. Sheila tells him it's a high-interest credit card and suggests a card with a lower interest rate because Mike has a good credit score. Mike is confused about interest rates on credit cards. He doesn't know how to evaluate credit cards for cash back, balance transfer, and zero interest. Mike has a lot to learn about these cards.

Let's help Mike understand credit cards and how to select the card that is the best for his use.

Credit cards have features that will affect what Mike will pay when he uses the card. Mike decided to spend some time researching various types of credit cards before choosing one. Sheila showed Mike how to evaluate credit cards. She talked about the factors to understand:

1) Annual Percentage Rate *(APR)*

The interest rate charged on a credit card is the annual interest charged on the credit card if Mike does not pay off the credit card balance at the end of the month. Interest payments on a credit card purchase means that the item purchased on a card is charged interest, which increases the balance on the card. When Mike pays off the credit card balance each month, he will not pay interest payments to the credit card company.

2) **Annual Fee**

The annual fee is the fee that credit card companies charge to use the credit card for purchases made for one year. When Mike evaluates credit cards, he should be asking if a credit card has an annual fee. Some credit cards do not charge an annual fee. Those cards may be a better deal, but Mike should look at all the components of a credit card to see what card is best for him.

3) **Cash or Balance Transfer to the Credit Card**

A balance transfer means you can move the credit card balance from another credit card or loan to the new credit card. Mike will have to ask if the card he's considering has a cash or balance transfer option. What is the interest rate on the balance transfer? What will the transaction fee be to do a balance transfer? Would Mike be able to write a check for cash using the credit card?

4) **Cash Back and/or Points on a Purchase**

Some credit cards offer cash back for every dollar charged on the credit card. Cards may also offer points for every credit card purchase. A card with a cash back feature will accumulate the amounts that were charged on the credit card and offer the cardholder a cash bonus or points toward a purchase. Points can be used to purchase travel, gift cards or cash towards paying off the credit card. Mike will want to consider the points or cash back on a card, and the amount of points or cash for each dollar spent on the card. Each credit card has its own offering regarding cash and points given for purchases. The cards with the most points or cash may be a better deal.

5) **Foreign Transaction Fees**

Some credit cards don't charge fees for using the card in other countries. If you travel overseas frequently for work or pleasure, you'll want to know whether your credit card charges a foreign transaction fee when you use the card out of the U.S. The fee is usually a percentage of the purchase amount. This fee adds additional cost to your purchase when you buy something overseas. Most credit cards will calculate the daily exchange rate for the value of the purchase. This means that if you bought an item in a country that uses Euros, the credit card company will convert the Euro cost into your currency, e.g., dollars. You will see the purchase on your credit card statement in dollars, not Euros.

> **“** If you travel overseas frequently, try to find a credit card that doesn't charge fees for purchases you make out of the U.S. **”**

Credit cards and bank savings accounts work in opposite ways. The savings account accrues interest on your money, so over time, your savings will grow because interest dividends are added to your bank balance. You are making money.

Credit card interest accrues on your credit card balance. If you don't pay off the credit card, the interest will accrue, and you will have to pay the interest to the bank for the privileges of borrowing the money by using the credit card. You are paying out money, not making money. Another way to look at this is that you end up paying more than the cost of a meal or a purchase if you don't pay off your credit card in full each month. You must consider the interest you're paying if you are maintaining a balance on your credit card bill.

Have you wondered how long it would take to pay off a credit card if you started buying things and charging them to a credit card, and increased the balance on the credit card?

How important is the interest rate on the credit card?

Let's give an example:

Mike has a credit card with Visa which has a credit card limit of $5,000.

Mike needs a new refrigerator because his is broken and repairing it would not be cost effective. A new refrigerator costs $2,000. Mike has also looked at used and refurbished refrigerators online and in reseller stores. He can buy a used one for $600. Mike decided he wants to buy a new one because the company offers a warranty which means it will repair the refrigerator if the appliance breaks down. However, Mike does not have the cash in the bank to buy the refrigerator with cash or debit card. So, he charges the new refrigerator to a credit card.

The first thing Mike should think about is whether he has the money to pay off the credit card purchase at the end of the month when it's due. If he does not, he should think about how many months it will take to pay off the refrigerator. When he knows this, he can then put that money in his budget to pay off the refrigerator in the number of months that he planned for in his budget.

His credit card statement, after the purchase of the refrigerator, looks like this:

Mike's Credit Card
Available credit limit: $5,000
Purchase refrigerator at Acme Company: $2,000
Total credit card balance: $2,000

Interest rate: 21% Annual interest rate
Cash back bonus on the card: 1% cash back for all purchases
The annual interest rate is 21%.

The simplest way to understand the interest rate on a credit card is to think that the higher the interest rate, the more money you will owe the credit card company if you don't pay off the credit card by the monthly due date.

If you pay off the balance by the due date, your interest payment on the credit card will be zero. However, if you do not pay off the credit card, your credit card interest will accrue and be added to the balance on the credit card, increasing the amount you owe. Think of interest paid as a loan fee for every month you don't pay off the credit card.

> 66 Think of interest paid as a loan fee for every month you don't pay off the credit card. 99

If you can pay off a credit card at the end of every month, you will save money by paying low or no interest payments on your credit card bill.

Paying off the credit card at the end of each month when it's due is the cheapest way to use credit. This means that you get to use someone else's money *(the credit card company's)* for free for thirty days.

Every month if you carry a balance on the credit card, you will pay 1/12 of the annual interest rate on the credit card balance. It looks like this:

21% interest annually / 12 months = 1.75% interest paid per month.
Month 1 is 1.75% times the $2,000 price of the refrigerator equals $35 in interest payment due.
.0175 X $2,000 = $35

If Mike did not make a payment on the refrigerator, the new balance on the credit card would be the $2,000 plus one month of interest, $35, which adds up to $2,035.

I recommend that you shop for interest rates on credit cards and loans to find one with a lower interest rate.

Let's take a look:

> Interest accrued on a $2,000 refrigerator at **21% APR** for one year: $420.
> Interest accrued on a $2,000 refrigerator at **6% APR** for one year: $120.

The 6% credit card rate charges less interest than the 21% credit card rate. The lower interest rate saves the credit card holder $300 per year in interest payments if the credit card was not paid off at the end of the month or soon after the refrigerator purchase.

Imagine what you can do with $300 saved in credit card interest. It can help you buy something else, or you can put it into savings. And if you paid off the $2,000 at the end of the month, you would owe $0 in credit card interest.

The cash back feature on Mike's credit card is also important. One percent cash back means that when Mike purchases the refrigerator, he will accrue 1% X $2,000 refrigerator = $20 cash back or points. He can use the cash back amount to put into savings to save for his next purchase.

Many people advise you not to buy anything on a credit card if you can't pay it off in full when the bill comes in. For instance, Mike could have bought a used refrigerator at a much cheaper price ($600) that he could pay off at the end of the month. Then he wouldn't have to go into debt for the refrigerator. This plan works well if you're disciplined about your spending, and you have a savings account or money set aside from your earnings to pay off a credit card bill at the end of the month.

Credit Card Balance Transfer: Does It Add Up?

You open your mail, and a letter tells you that you are eligible for a balance transfer from another credit card or loan to your credit card with zero percent interest!

The letter proudly says, ***"Save on interest when you consolidate high-interest-rate credit card balances."***

Sounds great, right?

You read the terms of the balance transfer offer, and it says:

A. Zero percent interest for twelve months on balance transfers.

B. Transfer fee of 3% on all transfers.

C. Must pay minimum monthly payment during the term of the promotional offer.

D. After the zero percent offer ends, the remaining balance will be charged 22.99% annual interest rate.

E. This card has no annual fee.

Balance transfers require that you transfer the credit card balance from another credit card or loan to the card that is offering the balance transfer promotion. Sometimes the offer will let you write a balance transfer check for anything you want. The balance transfer option will let you add debt to your card up to the credit limit that you have on the card.

Sally is interested in this offer, but she wants to make sure the deal makes sense for her. Let's help Sally figure out if the balance transfer deal is worth it.

Sally is currently paying 15.99% APR on her current card, CARD A.

Her credit card balance on the card is $9,300. She is not paying an annual fee to use this card.

She is receiving 1% cash back on the card. For every purchase she makes, she receives the 1% credit on her credit card account. The credit may be credit on her existing balance on her card, points for travel, or points to buy gift cards, etc.

CARD B offers a balance transfer rate of 0%. She has a zero balance on CARD B. Her APR rate is 22.99% on the card. This card has no annual fee to use the card.

First, we ask Sally some questions:

1) Will she be able to **pay off** the $9,300 in twelve months, the term for free interest on Card B?

2) What is the credit limit for Card B? Will she be able to **move all the debt from Card A to Card B?**

3) What does the 3% **transfer fee cost** her to move the debt over from CARD A to CARD B?

4) What is the **interest rate difference** between the two credit cards?

5) What is the **cash back or points** she receives if she uses each card?

6) Is there an **annual fee** the credit card company charges to use the credit card?

Answer 1) No, she cannot pay off the balance in twelve months. If she cannot pay it off in twelve months, she will be paying interest on the credit card balance on CARD B after month twelve when the free interest rate expires.

Answer 2) She has a $10,000 credit card limit on Card B. So, the $9,300 from CARD A can transfer to CARD B without going over the CARD B credit limit.

Answer 3) To figure out the fee to transfer a balance, we multiply 3% by the balance transfer amount, which she says is $9,300.

3% = .03, so .03 X $9,300 = $279 in balance transfer fees. The balance transfer fee will be added to the $9,300 balance that transfers from CARD A to CARD B.

Answer 4) The difference in credit card interest in CARD A is 15.99%. CARD B interest rate is 22.99%. The difference in interest rates is 22.99 – 15.99 = 7%.

Answer 5) Both credit cards have a 1% cash back when purchases are made on the card.

Answer 6) Both credit cards have a zero annual fee to use the card.

Let's plug Sally's interest rates and fees into Table 7.1:

Table 7.1 Sally's Credit Card Comparison – Year 1

Year 1	CARD A	CARD B	Interest Cost
Annual Interest Rate	15.99%	22.99%	
Monthly Interest Rate	.013325	.018333	
Balance Transfer Amount	$9,300	$9,300	
Annual Interest Paid	$1,487.07	0	$1,487.07
Fees Paid for Balance Transfer		$279	+$279
Cost to Sally – Year 1	$1,487.07	$279	-$1,208.07

In Year 1, it looks like the balance transfer option for Sally will save money because she will pay $279 to transfer her debt to CARD B but would be paying $1,487 in interest if she kept the debt on CARD A. So, transferring the balance from Card B to Card A saves Sally $1,208.07

in the first year, because she is not paying interest on her credit card balance. She will only pay the transfer fee of $279.

Let's assume Sally makes the balance transfer to CARD B. During the next twelve months, she pays down CARD B's balance from $9,300 to a balance of $6,000. After the twelve-month free interest period, CARD B's rate increases to 22.99%.

Both cards have a 1% cash back feature, so using either CARD A or CARD B will give cash back or points on the amount charged.

These calculations are for quick, simple use. We are multiplying the credit card balance times the annual interest rate. For most credit cards, the company charges 1/12 of the annual interest to the credit card balance each month.

What is Sally paying now in year 2 for interest? Table 7.2 shows the balance if she kept Card A and did not transfer the balance versus Card B where she transferred the credit card balance. We assume she pays down the credit card balance to $6,000 by the start of year 2.

Table 7.2 Sally's Cost of Balance Transfer – Year 2

Year 2	CARD A	CARD B	Interest Cost
Annual Interest Rate	15.99%	22.99%	
Monthly Interest Rate	.013325	.018333	
Balance Transfer Amount	$6,000	$6,000	
Annual Interest Paid	$959.40	$1,379.40	
Fees Paid for Balance Transfers		0	
Cost to Sally – Year 2	$959.40	$1,379.40	$420

At the start of Year 2, Sally will be paying more interest on her credit card balance because the interest paid is higher on CARD B than CARD A.

She will be paying $1,379.40 *(Card B Interest)* minus $959.40 *(Card A interest)* = $420 more per year in interest in Year 2. We didn't include the additional payments she made in Year 2 to pay down her credit card in year 2. This table assumes she kept a $6,000 balance throughout the year for simple math.

You can use the Year 2 table to compare two credit cards that you already have to figure out the interest you are paying on each one for a year. Seeing interest payments accrued on your credit card bill is no fun. Knowing how much you pay in interest may help you figure out how to get rid of the credit card debt.

Some wise math hacks suggest that you compare your credit card interest rates using a table like the one I've used. They then chose to pay off the highest interest-rate card or debt first. They then pay down the next highest interest rate card or loan. This is how they make progress in paying off their debt.

Other math hacks say to pay off the smallest credit card balance first and then pay off the next highest credit card balance. Either plan, paying off the highest credit card interest account first, or paying off the lowest credit card balance first, will help you eliminate debt. Paying off your credit card balances, one card at a time, may provide extra money each month to pay for other expenses or deposit into a savings account.

If you have a credit card balance each month like Sally has, you should call the credit card company and ask for a reduced interest rate on the card or a special promotional interest rate. You may be pleasantly surprised because credit card companies usually want you to keep using their cards so they will often offer special promotions if you ask what options are available. Asking for lower interest rates and getting a new reduced rate from the credit card company gives you freedom. You're saving on interest payments, which puts more money in your pocket, or you can apply the money saved to help pay off the credit card faster by applying the interest savings to pay down the credit card balance.

Another strategy is to take the savings you would have otherwise spent and transfer it to your savings account. Keep track of this! You will see that your savings will start growing aside from any other monthly savings you do. Make it fun so it doesn't seem like a chore—and then reward yourself or your family.

Let's use the example in Table 7.2. If you had an interest rate of 22.99% and after you asked the bank for a reduced interest rate, they agreed and gave you 15.99%. How much can you save per month on interest payments? If you had a credit card balance of $6,000 on the credit card, for example, you could save: $1,379.40 minus $959.40 = $420 per year. Divide $420 by twelve months to get $35 per month. The $35 per month can be used to pay extra money towards the monthly credit card payment.

Review Your Credit Card Bill For Fraudulent Purchases

Review your credit card statement every month to ensure the charges are correct. Doing so can help you identify the occasional double charge and even fraudulent charges. If you find fraudulent charges or other errors, call the bank or credit card issuer immediately to dispute the charges.

> ❝ Review your credit card statement every month to ensure the charges are correct. Doing so can help you identify the occasional double charge and even fraudulent charges. ❞

Banks and credit card issuers will help you stop fraudulent use of your credit card. After you call them and report the fraudulent use, they will close your existing card account and issue you a new card, with a new credit card number. They will review and research the fraudulent charges to determine whether they were fraudulent and discuss the results with you.

Use a credit card rather than a debit card when purchasing items in stores and online. If a fraudulent purchase is made using your credit card, the credit card company can close the card and review the charges.

A debit card, however, is linked to your checking or savings account. A fraudster can make purchases using your debit card information and reduce your checking or savings account balance to zero. It is more time consuming and a hassle to recover from fraudulent debit card withdrawals from a checking or savings account. First, the checking or savings account must be closed to stop the withdrawals. Closing a bank account is problematic if the bank account is your primary bank account, and you deposit or spend money from the account daily. Second, all automatic monthly payments to creditors that you set up for the account will have to be re-entered into the online bank system for the new bank account.

To avoid potential fraudulent withdrawals from your bank account, use credit cards to make purchases online or in stores. Use the debit card for ATM withdrawals only.

Where To Put Your Savings: Certificate of Deposit, Money Market Account, Savings Account

When you've saved up money by comparing prices and buying everyday items like groceries, or saved in interest by paying off debit, use the Money Keeping Journal or a phone app to track the amount you've saved. It's motivating to see how much you have saved by tracking it daily! Every day you save on a purchase, move the money saved out of your checking account and into a savings account. After a month or two, move the money to a money market or investment account that does not link to your checking account. Then it will be harder to tap into the money, which will help you save even more.

Let's talk about different types of savings accounts.

Traditional Savings Account

This type of account can be opened at any bank or financial institution. It can be attached to a checking account if needed. It holds your savings, and it's easy to add or withdraw money using a debit card that the bank will give you when you open a savings account. It usually does not pay above market interest on your money. A savings account can be used as you start your money-keeping journey. After you have saved $500 or more, transfer your savings to other types of bank accounts that offer higher interest rates to help your money grow faster.

Certificate of Deposit (CD)

This type of account has a minimum amount required to be invested and features a fixed term for the deposit. This means that when you put your money in this account, you cannot withdraw it until the term is up. For example, a CD with a term of twelve months means you cannot withdraw the money for twelve months. If you do, you are penalized with a fee for early withdrawal. CDs are best for times when you will not need the money before the end of the term of the CD.

Money Market Account

This bank account allows you to add money to the account and withdraw money that you need. It pays an interest rate on your money that is usually greater than the interest paid on a savings account. A money market account may have a minimum balance requirement to open and maintain the account.

It's important to consider which type of account -- a savings account, CD, or a money market account – is right for you. What interest rate will you be earning? Does the interest rate keep up with the rate of inflation?

Inflation – How Does It Affect Your Savings

You've probably heard the word inflation on the news or read about it in a newspaper at some point. Inflation is a factor calculated by the U.S. government to measure how quickly prices are increasing in our economy.

During a high inflation economy, it's critical to look at the money you have in investments and in a bank. Look at the interest rate you are receiving from the bank and compare it to the inflation rate that the U.S. government declares each month. For example, Sharon has a savings account earning 1% interest per year. She also has a credit card with an outstanding balance. She is paying 18.99% on the credit card balance. For this example, the annual inflation rate is 4%.

It looks like Sharon's savings account *(1% interest)* is not keeping up with the rate of inflation *(4%)*. She is receiving 1% interest but is losing the value of her money given a high inflation rate of 4%. She earns 1% but is losing the value of her savings due to inflation of 4%. One percent earned minus 4% inflation = 3% loss in the value of her money each year. Sharon decides to look at other investments that earn more interest or evaluate if it makes sense to pay off a credit card or loan, which charges a higher interest rate. It's something you should consider periodically to make certain you're maximizing your savings and investments.

Check out the amount you are receiving in interest on your savings and money market accounts. Review your credit card balances and know the interest rate you are being charged. Then decide if the low-interest-rate savings can be used to pay off the high-interest-rate credit cards. If you pay off your credit cards each month, then look for a savings or investment account that pays a higher rate of interest on your money. Research the options available that best suit your needs.

> 66 Decide if low-interest-rate savings can be used to pay off the high-interest-rate credit cards. 99

Brokerage Accounts

When you have saved at least $1,000 in your savings account, consider talking to a reputable investment advisor. Look into investment accounts as well. You or your trusted investment advisor will have to do research into the investment to determine if the higher risk associated with the investment is appropriate for you.

An investment has a higher risk if the investment can drop in value below what you paid for it. The investment advisors call this the risk-reward threshold or ratio. Risk-reward is important because you -- the investor -- can decide the level of risk you will take *(potential loss of money)* vs. the reward you can gain *(potential gain in value)*.

Some stocks generate a dividend, which is money paid to you based on the company's profitability. Other stocks do not generate a dividend. They increase or decrease in value, and as an investor, you have to decide whether the stock is worth buying. You'll have to do some research to evaluate the ability of the stock to grow in value, based on how profitable the company is. You may want to get financial advice about stocks from an experienced and reputable professional before investing in them.

Emergency Savings and Saving for Holiday Shopping or Trips

You start saving money by wisely purchasing items and deposit the money in a bank account. It is important to plan for unexpected events like emergencies and have money for these unexpected events.

Experts recommend that you save three to six months of expenses for emergencies in a savings account or money market fund. You will have the savings to pay monthly expenses during untimely events such as layoffs, disasters, unexpected large expenses, or illness.

Another expense to budget for is holiday shopping and taking a vacation or trip to visit family. In Chapter 10, we discuss how to prepare a budget for holiday shopping, vacations and setting a monthly budget.

Deciding what you will invest in, a bank deposit account, stocks, bonds, or other investments like real estate will be your choice as you search for investments that meet your risk reward threshold.

Key Money-Saving Tips

1) Use a Money Keeping Journal and note the savings you have found in the journal.

2) Move the money saved each week to a savings account or money market account.

3) When you have saved up at least $500, move that money to a higher interest-bearing account.

4) Compare your savings to the remaining credit card, car loan or other debt balance. Determine whether using savings to pay off a high-interest rate debt will help you reduce your monthly expenses.

5) Review interest rates on credit cards and balance transfer offers to find the best one for you.

6) Do the math and find the cost of a balance transfer from one credit card to another. Pick a balance transfer program only if it works for you.

7) Remember, using savings to pay off credit cards may make sense, if the savings interest rate is lower than the credit card interest rate.

8) Review your credit card statement every month to ensure the charges look correct. Doing so can help you identify the occasional double charge and even fraudulent charges.

Chapter 8

Save Thousands When Buying a Car

"Wish not so much to live long as to live well."

-Benjamin Franklin

Let's talk about buying a car, boat, or other expensive items. We will walk through the purchase of a car with Trina and Leo.

Do you have cash available to buy a car, boat, or other durable thing? Paying cash allows you to save thousands of dollars in interest payments that you would otherwise have to pay the bank when you take out a loan to buy a car or boat or another big-ticket item.

Buying a Car Using a Loan

Let's say we see a car we want to buy. We don't have the cash to buy it. So, we will take out a loan. The price of the car is good, and the loan rate appears to be reasonable. How can we research ahead of time to buy the car and save thousands of dollars?

Lease vs. Purchase

A car dealership may suggest that you lease a car, rather than purchasing it. If you have a business, the car lease payment may be deductible on your taxes. Ask your tax advisor about vehicle expense deductibility.

However, you will have to turn the car in after the lease period ends and choose another vehicle to lease. In effect, you will always be making car payments since you are not paying off the car.

Conversely, if you take out a loan to buy a car, you may be able to pay off the car loan and have no further payments! In the following example, Trina and Leo do not own businesses and have decided to take out loans for their cars.

A Story of Trina and Leo and the Auto Dealership

The car dealership salesperson, Harry, helps customers find a car that works well for their purposes. Let's look at the stories of Trina and Leo who each want to purchase a vehicle. Both individuals will be taking out a loan to buy their cars.

Trina wants to buy a new car that will have room for her golf clubs and space for her dog kennel, where she keeps her dog, Fido, when she is driving around town. The vehicle that she has been driving has had multiple engine problems and is breaking down every other month. Trina's car is paid off, so she has no outstanding loan on the car. Trina has spent thousands on car repairs and has decided that the money she is spending on repairs could be put into a new car as car payments. She decided that vehicle reliability is more important than a paid-off car.

She looks at a sports utility vehicle *(SUV)* that is large enough for her stuff. She has looked online on various websites and has read various vehicle quality reports to find the make and model of a vehicle that has great quality and a reasonable price.

She waits until the dealership closes, then walks the car lot looking for the price of the vehicle she likes on the car dealership lot. She doesn't want to be bothered by salespeople at this time. Trina knows the prices of similar cars. She finds other car dealerships and their price online; she asks her wholesale warehouse the price of the car she wants.

A wholesale warehouse is a members-only store that sells food, clothing, appliances and can order a new car for customers. These *"clubs"* tell you that they can save you money if you buy a car through them, with no haggling or negotiating. They are the middleman between the car dealer and you. Sometimes they can negotiate a good deal, and sometimes you can negotiate a better deal on your own with the car dealership directly.

Trina also shopped around for used cars like her model to see what it would cost if she bought a used car. She found out that the used car price for the model of car she wants is only $3,000 less than a new car. She decides to pay a little more for a new car that will include vehicle warranties to pay for repairs if anything breaks down.

> ## ★ Math Hack Secret ★
>
> When I am negotiating a price for a new car, I like to order a true car value report. Some companies sell online reports which shows the wholesale price and the retail price of the car. The cost of this report is reasonable as it may enable you to save substantially on your car purchase. The report shows the wholesale value of the car and wholesale price for all the car options the car has. The report also shows the retail asking price for the car and the retail price of the options.

I buy the report and compare the wholesale cost to the sticker price on the vehicle on the car lot. Then I do the math and figure out the price that is between the wholesale price and the suggested retail price of the car. I set my negotiating price above the wholesale price but lower than the retail price. If you can find this report online, order it and read it before you negotiate a car deal.

Trina is ready to visit the dealership, armed with various vehicle reports, actual purchase prices, sales prices of vehicles at wholesale warehouses, and the prices of upgraded features of the car. She has visited multiple banks and written down their loan rates for new cars, so she knows what interest rate she can get based on her credit score. She asked the bank and knew the estimated loan payment she can expect, and she is ready to negotiate a deal with the car dealership.

Harry, the car dealership salesman, approaches Trina on the car lot as she walks toward the car she had already checked out when the dealership was closed. She test drives the car to make sure it drives the way she wants because secretly she has a lead foot and speeds around! She wants to make sure the car will stop quickly, do *"U"* turns well, and accelerates quickly. She asks if the dealership will take a price below the vehicle sticker price. She has already priced out the same or similar vehicle on other car lots, so she knows the average prices for the vehicles.

However, Harry wants Trina to pay full price plus some because he makes more money if she pays more for the car. He also wants to promote the dealership's financing deals, and their extended warranties, because he makes money by promoting the financing and warranty program, too.

There are additional costs when you're purchasing a new car including:

1) The vehicle cost before upgraded equipment on the vehicle is added,

2) The upgrade costs – blind spot indicator, larger wheels, more powerful engine, etc.

3) Extended vehicle repair warranties,

4) Other items like dent repair, clear coat on the car, tire repair, etc.

5) Interest rate and the length of the loan if you want to finance the car.

After Trina test drives the car, Harry asks Trina to step inside the dealership office so they can make a deal on the SUV. Harry drives the SUV up to the front of the lot by the sales office so Trina can see it through the window. Harry hopes that Trina will get excited looking at it and see it as hers as she is negotiating a price and terms. Also, Trina drove to the dealership in her old Honda. Harry says that Trina may be able to trade in her car and get trade-in money to reduce the price of her new car. Some mechanic wants to take the keys from Trina and drive her car to the back lot, where she can't see it anymore. Harry says they will drive it to the back so they can check it out for a price to offer Trina for her car.

Harry asks the question, *"How much do you want to pay for your monthly payment on this car?"*

Dealers ask this question s<u>o they can rip you off and make more money for themselves!</u>

Don't fall for it. They hope that you hate math enough to be clueless about how they calculate your loan and the rate they charge. Know the monthly payment you can afford **before** you go to a car dealer. **DO NOT tell them your desired monthly payment.**

You'll want to negotiate a price, loan, and terms that are the best deal, not pay more. Dealers may find a way to load in additional costs on the sales contract so your total cost is more than you should be paying.

How do you know what a good monthly payment would be for you, that you can calculate before you go to a dealership?

Let's figure out what your desired monthly payment will be using any loan app you can get online. You can also check many websites that have payment calculators that you can use for free.

NOTE: I like to use finance loan apps like Bankrate.com and KBB.com

Let's check out various financing plans.

> Price of the car + sales tax = $30,000
> Interest rate that the bank offers for the loan: 6%
> What is your monthly payment?

$30,000 is called the principal balance – the total price of the car including tax and all options.

.06 is the Interest rate *(I)* or 6%. This is the interest rate offered by some banks or lenders. You know the best *(lowest rate)* because you called or visited the banks to find the rates offered based on your credit score.

> 5-year loan term -- 5-year loan times number of payments per year *(12 months)* = 60 monthly payments

Type these numbers into the blanks on the app and then the app or website will then solve for payment:

> Solve for monthly payment also known as PV *(present value)* = $579.98

Can you afford the monthly payment you calculated? If not, reduce the price of the car by finding one with fewer upgrades or picking a different model, add sales tax, and calculate it again.

Maybe a six- or seven-year loan would work better if it were offered?

Maybe a car with fewer vehicle extras and a less expensive price?

Maybe a used car with low miles and in good condition will work?

Let's do the math and figure out what the car payment would be for a $20,000 car loan at 6% interest and a six-year loan term.

> $20,000 = price of the car including tax
> .06 = Interest *(I)* 6% loan interest annually
> 6-year loan term *(6 X 12 = 72 car payments total)*
> The loan payment would be $331 per month for seventy-two months.

If this is a difficult calculation for you, go to your bank and ask a representative to figure out loan payments for the price of a car you are looking at. Know that the loan payment will increase for every dollar increase in the price of a car that you buy.

★ Math Hack Secret ★

Get a quote from a bank or lender for a car loan that works for you. Keep it on hand when you visit a dealership. The dealer may try to charge a higher rate of interest if the dealer finances your loan. Since you have another loan quote from your lender, you may be able to negotiate a better loan rate with the car dealership. The dealer may compete with your current lender to offer you a better interest rate, to encourage you to finance the car with them.

You will already know your monthly loan payment because the bank provided that information in the loan quote to you. Knowing your loan rate and terms helps you because the dealer can't ask, *"How much do you want to pay per month?"* You will already know the interest rate, loan terms, and car price that fits your budget.

Trina has done her homework by:

1) Researching the average sales price that other people in her area paid for this car,

2) Comparing the price of cars from multiple dealerships, warehouse stores, and used car stores,

3) Figuring out her desired car payment *(Price, interest rate, term of the loan)*,

4) Determining how much the upgrades and options cost on a new car,

5) Learning what the current interest rates are for vehicle loans, both new and used,

6) Confirming her credit score *(FICO)* and the interest rate she could get from various banks,

7) Calculating how much her car is worth – trading in the car to the dealership, selling it to a car broker, or selling it to a private party *(selling it herself)*,

8) Comparing the cost of extended warranties available and what parts and labor the warranties cover.

Harry is not prepared to start dealing with Trina, who has come equipped with the tools and knowledge needed to buy this particular car. Trina states a price she will pay for the car including the upgrades on the car. Harry says he will have to ask his manager and disappears for thirty minutes.

Trina is tired of waiting for half an hour, because her time is valuable, and decides to leave the dealership. As she passes the hallway, she notices Harry is just lingering in the hallway, not in his sales manager's office. He was hoping that Trina would want the car so much that she would take it at the full price after waiting so long for him to return!

Trina is angry with Harry and asks the manager for another sales-person to help her, someone who won't waste her time. The sales manager talks to Trina and can see that Trina is prepared to walk out. He wants to help Trina. All the salespeople in the dealership look down their noses and shame Harry, who really messed up by treating Trina disrespectfully.

The same day Trina is at the dealership, Leo walks into the auto deal-ership. He is *"just looking"* but finds a cool Jeep he likes. His current vehicle is having mechanical issues, and he is tired of driving it into the auto shop and paying for car repairs, like Trina.

Harry pops up from behind a car near Leo, walks out toward Leo from behind the car, and asks if he can help Leo. Harry asks Leo questions to find out how much research he has done on the car. Since Leo did not do the research that Trina did, Leo will probably pay too much for the car.

Harry allows Leo to test drive the Jeep. Harry will tell Leo how sharp he looks when he is driving the car. Harry asks Leo if the auto repair team can take his old car into the back lot to price it out for trade-in value. Leo agrees. But Leo does not know the value of his car because he did not research his car's resale value either.

Harry suggests an auto loan and terms, using the dealership's finance team. But Leo does not know his FICO credit score, which determines the interest rate the bank will charge for the car loan. Leo also does not know the current lowest interest rate he could get for the loan, because he did not shop around at other lenders and banks and ask what their interest rates were.

Leo likes the Jeep; it's white, his favorite color. Leo did not know what Trina knew about wholesale warehouse car sellers. Below is useful in-formation about these other places to buy a new car. Then we will get back to Trina and Leo's deals and how their deals compare to each other.

Treat your Wholesale Warehouse Seller the Same as You Would a Car Dealership

Some credit unions, wholesale warehouse stores, and online car dealers may tell you they have the best deal on vehicles. They may say they beat out the middleman and will save you money because you pay less.

You may think that you can avoid negotiating with a dealership and still get the best price. Some buyers are uncomfortable trying to buy a car from a hungry salesperson like Harry at a car dealership.

However, it's your money so you should ask yourself whether you want to pay for a car and find out later your neighbor got the same car for less, or he got some free floor mats and window treatments, and paid less than you? He also negotiated a better interest rate on the loan than you, so he is saving money on a monthly car payment. You'd probably be annoyed at yourself for not saving money or getting the best possible deal.

Always compare the wholesale car warehouses with the dealerships' prices. The car dealership has no middleman, so a dealer can sometimes negotiate a better deal than the wholesaler, who IS the middleman between you and the dealership.

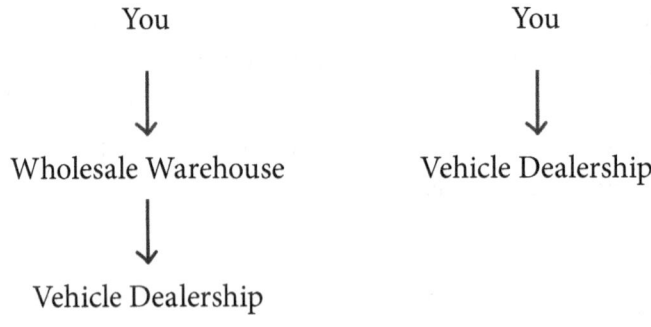

Trina's Deal and Leo's Deal

Let's do the math to find out how well Trina did in her negotiation for a car compared to Leo. The sales manager convinces Trina to come back to the negotiation table after apologizing profusely for Harry leaving her in the lobby alone for thirty minutes.

Trina's Deal Price

The car she liked was $30,000. She knows other new cars with similar upgraded features as the one she likes in this sales lot sold for $27,000.

She priced out the car with similar features on the warehouse sites and at other dealerships in other states, so she knows the approximate cost should be $27,000.

She offered $27,000 to the dealership for the new car.

$30,000 *(price on the car)* - $27,000 her offer = $3,000 savings on a car if she gets the deal.

Interest Rate

Trina has shopped around and knows that for her credit score, she can get a 4.95% interest rate loan for a five-year term.

She tells the finance manager that she wants a 4.95% loan and asks the dealership to offer her a rate that will beat her bank's rate where she has received a car loan payment quote. The sales manager, Mike, knows his dealership usually charges 7% to customers who do not negotiate the interest rate for a car.

7% *(dealership interest rate)* – 4.95% *(Trina's bank interest rate)* = 2.05% savings in the interest rate. Mike calls the vehicle lenders that he works with, and one of them will offer Trina the 4.95% interest rate, to match her bank's car loan rate.

Extended Warranty

Trina wants an extended warranty on the car. She usually drives the same car for ten or more years and approximately 4,000 miles a year. The standard manufacturer's warranty for this car is five years *(sixty months)* or 60,000 miles, whichever comes first. She is looking for a warranty that will cover her car repairs for ten years, if possible. She has researched the average price to purchase an extended vehicle warranty, the total mileage included, and the car parts and labor costs covered by the warranty during the extended warranty period.

Her model of SUV includes a manufacturer's warranty of five years or 60,000 miles. If Trina buys an extended warranty, she will add another five years or 60,000 miles to the manufacturer warranty, which results in a ten-year or a 120,000-mile warranty. She has decided to buy an extended warranty, because she plans to keep the car for ten years and will be driving less than 120,000 miles during that time.

Other Additional Items

She asks the dealership to add in rubber floor mats as part of the deal and they agree, saving her $400.

She does not let Mike, the sales manager, take her existing car and drive it to the service shop at the back of the building. She instead asks Mike to calculate the price the dealer will offer her for her car. She already priced the value of the car online if she sold it to another company or another dealer. She knows she can sell it to another dealer or a wholesale company for $8,000.

Trina knows if the dealership won't offer a good price to buy the new car, she will walk out and drive her Honda back home, as Mike pleads with her to change her mind.

★ **Math Hack Secret** ★

Always be ready to walk out of a dealership if the dealer isn't negotiating a deal you feel good about.

After some negotiating, the dealership offers Trina this deal:

$28,000 is the price the dealership offers for the new car.

It's $1,000 more than she offered, but they would provide all car maintenance and repairs in one location. She decides it's acceptable to pay $1,000 more, but in exchange for paying $1,000 more, she asks for free upgrades like floor mats, window tint, and tire replacement. The sales manager reluctantly agrees.

4.95% interest rate – The dealership matches the interest rate from her bank. Remember, you must be prepared and have a rate approved by your bank first, for the dealership to shop and match the interest rate quote you received.

Rubber floor mats – She asked them to add them to the car for free.

Extended warranty $4,000 – their price matched other warranty companies.

The dealer offered to pay her $5,000 for her existing Honda.

Mike said that it's better to trade in a car because of all the sales tax she would save on the new car. Have you ever heard a car dealer say that to you?

Is that statement true?

Let's look at what is really happening: the $5,000 credit for her Honda trade-in would be deducted from the price of the new car, before sales tax is calculated. I don't think some people understand how much or little this saves in sales tax.

Below is the math showing Trina's sales tax savings if she traded in the old car vs. selling her old car to another party, not the car dealership.

Total Cost if Trina Traded in her Honda to the Dealership

$ 28,000 – Car price
$ 4,000 – Extended vehicle warranty
$ 32,000 – Total price
– $ 5,000 – Minus trade-in value from Trina's Honda
$ 27,000 – Price of new car minus trade-in before tax
$ 2,430 – Add sales tax at 9%
$ 29,430 – Total cost of the car with a vehicle trade-in

Cost of the car without her Honda Trade-In

$ 28,000 – Price of car before tax
$ 4,000 – Extended vehicle warranty
$ 32,000 – Total price
$ 2,880 – Add sales tax at 9%
$ 34,880 – Total cost of the car without a vehicle trade in

Trina's additional sales tax savings if she trades in the Honda are:

Without Honda trade-in – sales tax: $2,880
With Honda trade-in – sales tax: $2,430
Sales tax savings: $2,880 - $2,430 = $450

Trina would save $450 in sales tax if she traded in the Honda at the dealership. But let's assume the Honda is really worth $8,000 if she sold it to an online wholesale vehicle seller or to a private party. The dealership will buy it for $5,000, but the $8,000 sale looks like a good option. How much will Trina save if she sells her car to a private party?

Sell Honda to an outside party after Trina buys the new car

```
   $ 28,000  – Price of the new car
+ $   4,000  – Extended warranty
   $ 32,000  – Total price
   $   2,880 – Add sales tax at 9% (.09 * $32,000)
   $ 34,880  – Total cost of the car
–  $   8,000 – Sell Honda to wholesale dealer or private party
   $ 26,880  – Actual cost of the car after selling the Honda
```

It looks like Trina can save $29,430 *(cost of car with trade-in)* minus the cost of the car with a sale to a wholesaler $26,880, which saves $29,430 minus $26,880 equals **$2,550 in savings** by selling the Honda to the higher bidder at a wholesale or other car buying company. Since Trina knows how much her car is worth if she sold it to another company, the dealer may decide to give her the trade-in price she wants. So, you should ask what the dealer will offer for your car if you want to sell it anyway, ONLY if you already know the price you can get for the car by selling it to another company that buys used cars.

What is Trina's monthly car payment? Let's assume she sold her used car to another car dealer.

Trina's loan terms:

5 years
4.95% – Interest rate *(annual rate)*
$34,880 – Vehicle loan amount
Trina's payment will be $657.43 per month for five years or 60 months.

How much will Trina pay for the car over the five-year loan if she takes the full five years to pay it off? $657.43 X 60 payments = $39,445.79.

Leo's Car Deal

Price

$30,000 – He loved the car, didn't know the average selling price, and believed the dealer when he said he wouldn't take any money off the purchase price. So, he paid full price for the car. The vehicle asking price on Leo's car was the same price as the asking price of Trina's car, $30,000.

$30,000 car price – Leo didn't know he could negotiate things like floor mats, extended warranties, etc.

Leo decided not to trade in his car to the dealership. He sold it to a friend instead.

Extended Warranty

The dealership offered Leo a $4,000 extended warranty. He agreed to pay for the extended warranty. However, he did not think about how long he would keep the car, and if the extended warranty made sense. Leo usually kept a car for five years before selling it. He usually drove approximately 8,000 miles per year. The standard manufacturer's warranty for this car is five years (*60 months*) or 60,000 miles, whichever comes first. The extended warranty offered an additional five years (*sixty months*) or 60,000 miles to the manufacturer's warranty. So, Leo is buying a warranty to protect his car for ten years or 120 months. Why would he buy an extended warranty he is not expecting to use? Would you do it?

Other Additional Items

Leo paid for rubber floor mats for his vehicle: $400 for floor mats.

Leo's sales slip for the new car looked like this:

$ 30,000 – Car price
$ 4,000 – Extended Warranty for the car
$ 400 – Floor mats
$ 34,400 – Subtotal

$\underline{\$\ \ 3,096}$ – Sales tax at 9%
$ 37,496 – Price that Leo pays

Interest Rate

Leo didn't check out the car loan rate at other banks, so he is paying 10% interest on the car loan. This will cost Leo a lot of money in inter-est, even though he has good credit, like Trina. If Leo had shopped for car loans before visiting the dealership, he may have received an offer for a car loan, which charged 6%. Leo could then use the car loan offer to negotiate a lower interest rate with the dealership.

What is Leo's car payment?

$37,496 Car loan amount
10% interest
Five-year loan
Leo's car payment is: $796.68 per month for five years

What is the total cost of the car for Leo over five years, including the interest he paid on the loan?

Car Payments $796.68 X 60 months *(five years)* = $47,801 – Total cost of the car for Leo.

Trina is paying $657.43 per month and Leo is paying $796.68 per month, so Trina is saving $139.25 per month by negotiating her car deal.

Trina will be paying less interest over the five-year term on her loan because she will be paying $39,446 and Leo will be paying $47,801. Trina will be paying $8,355 less than Leo over the five years of the loan. They both found a car with the same retail price, $30,000, but Trina will be saving more because she researched car prices and interest rates to negotiate a car price and interest rate for the car loan, which was a better deal than Leo.

To summarize this car-buying adventure, if you do the homework and find out these important criteria before you go to the dealer, you will save money:

1) Average price of the car you want,

2) Interest rates that you can get from a few banks and lenders, and an estimated monthly payment you will pay,

3) Vehicle extended warranty price and what is included,

4) Extra car upgrades that you can request be included for free,

5) The value of your car if you sell it to a warehouse, dealership, wholesale dealer or direct buyer *(private party)*.

Armed with this information, you will be able to handle any pushy salesperson at any dealership or wholesale dealer. Being knowledgeable about these details will allow you to negotiate a great deal for yourself and your family.

Key Money-Saving Tips

1) The best way to negotiate for a car is to do your homework and research first. Then you can negotiate a deal with confidence.

2) If you take out a car loan, look at the interest rate you can get from your bank or lender so you can compare it to the loan offered by the auto dealership.

3) Price cars for sale at wholesale membership stores, fixed price car wholesale dealers, automobile dealerships, for sale by owner, and online websites for vehicles out of state. Some credit unions sell cars as well.

4) Don't be afraid to walk away from the car deal if it does not make sense to you.

Chapter 9

Buying a Home with a Mortgage Loan that Works for You

"We can't help everyone, but everyone can help someone."

-Ronald Reagan

Buying a home is probably the biggest investment you'll be making in your lifetime. Think about it. You are putting down hard-earned savings to buy a home! It's not a stock or bond. It's an investment that you and your family live in, possibly for years.

I call it an investment because you are investing money into an asset which becomes your home project. This is a big project. If you can maintain the home and improve it as you go, it creates value for you and your family.

Another reason I call it an investment is that if you obtain a fixed-rate mortgage on the property, you are protected from interest rate changes that occur in the overall economy.

Your mortgage payment will be the same, for principal and interest. The only changes in the payment will be for property tax increases, homeowners' insurance, and possibly homeowner association *(HOA)* fees if the home is located in a homeowner's association or co-op.

In most cases, if you can afford to buy a home, it's a better option than paying rent and experiencing increased rent payments as landlords may increase the rent each year. However, if you anticipate moving to another city or state within three years for a job change or other lifestyle change, renting for the short-term may make sense. In addition, if you can't qualify for a home because your credit score *(FICO)* is below the minimum score to qualify for a home loan, then renting makes sense.

In 2005, I was looking to buy a home. I had to sell my existing home because I wanted to move to a neighborhood that had a golf course nearby so I could golf there. At that time, the market was red-hot and homes on the market had multiple offers—and the home prices were increasing rapidly because of the high demand for houses.

At this time, people were quickly buying homes to rent out to others with no money down, no income earned, and no proof of funds – buyers bank balances in the bank. Interestingly, some lenders performed no credit check and required no verification of the buyer's income. The loan they were offering was called a Stated Income Loan.

Stated Income Loans work like this: you tell the lender you make $X income per year *(even if you don't)*, and they write that number down and tell you what mortgage you can qualify for.

A variable rate loan means that the interest rate would move up or down each year based on the interest rate in the financial market every year. An interest-only mortgage is a mortgage loan in which the buyer pays only the interest on the loan, not the principal balance, unless they want to pay principal and interest. The loan balance never drops if the borrower pays interest-only and no principal payment. Interest-only loans are discussed at the end of the chapter.

My realtor at the time referred me to a mortgage company so I called to discuss mortgages. The mortgage officer told me I could get a variable rate loan or a stated income loan. I asked about fixed-rate mortgages, because I wanted to know what fixed mortgage payment I would pay each month *(principal and interest each month)*.

The mortgage officer laughed at me, and I could hear the other mortgage people laughing in the background on the phone! He said to the other mortgage officers, ***"She wants a fixed-rate mortgage!"*** After the laughing subsided, he told me that no one gets a fixed-rate mortgage anymore. He said fixed-rate mortgages are old school. Everyone is taking out a variable rate mortgage, stated income mortgage, or an interest-only mortgage.

I thought to myself, I can't take a risk by assuming that the interest rates will remain the same. If the interest rates increase, so does my mortgage payment! I promptly ended the call with the mortgage officer and took out a fixed-rate mortgage with a bank, which had more conservative lending practices and offered fixed-rate mortgages.

In 2008, the whole housing market crashed. In Las Vegas, the house values decreased by up to 50 percent! Interest rates started climbing. The people who used the variable rate mortgage, stated income mortgage or the interest-only mortgage began to default as their mortgage payments increased and their property values decreased.

The people who bought rental properties had difficulty renting them because too many people bought rental homes thinking they could buy one with a zero down payment and a stated income variable rate loan. Too many homes for lease resulted in my city being flooded with rental homes with few tenants renting the properties. People who bought these homes to rent out had no money invested in their rental home, and no tenant to rent it. They defaulted on their mortgage as a foreclosure or sold the property as a short sale. In retrospect, the stated income loans were known as junk loans or sub-prime loans. The lenders did not screen the borrowers to make sure they could afford the homes.

Other home buyers bought homes, and they could not afford the mortgage payment. When the loan interest rate increased with the market, the mortgage payment increased as well. The buyers could not pay the increased mortgage payment and then defaulted on the loan. The banks foreclosed on many loans during that period. These loans caused the home market crash in 2008. View this as a cautionary tale: even if a lending practice is popular, it doesn't necessarily mean it's good practice overall or good for your financial situation.

> ★ **Math Hack Secret** ★
>
> Even if a lending practice is popular, it doesn't necessarily mean it's good practice overall or good for your financial situation.

At the end of this chapter, I will talk about the various types of mortgages to help you understand how they work.

You can decide whether to buy a home if you can afford it or you can choose to rent one. It's important to understand the financial implications over time of renting compared to buying a home. Let's watch how Joe and Sarah navigate the home buying or renting process.

Joe and Sarah's Options to Buy or Rent a Home

Joe wants to rent a home. He thinks that buying a home is like wearing cement shoes. He believes he will not have the freedom to move from home to home based on his needs. He can afford to buy a home but has decided against it.

His friend Sarah wants to buy a home. Sarah sees the possibility to build equity through home improvements and by paying down the mortgage to reduce the loan balance on her home.

Joe looks around town and finds a rental property to rent for $2,500 per month.

If Joe rents the property, he must pay the rent the landlord is asking. If the landlord increases the rent the following year, Joe will have to pay the new rent rate or move out to another home, if he can find one. Joe does not have rent security. He doesn't know what his rent payment will be in the future. So, Joe experiences rent risk.

Let's say that Joe rents the home for one year at $2,500 per month. Near the end of the lease, the landlord tells Joe that the rent will increase by 8%. Joe will have to calculate the new rent payment. Let's help Joe figure out the rent. His current rate, $2,500, will increase by 8%, so the word problem is: What is 8% of $2,500?

8% → .08

Rent $2,500 X .08 = $200. $200 is the increase in the rent that Joe will have to pay. What is the new rent payment for Joe? $2,500 + $200 = $2,700 per month.

Joe has to deal with rent risk because, as a renter, he has no control over the landlord's rent increases. Joe can decide whether he wants to continue renting from this landlord or find a new home to rent. Maybe he can find a home that has rent controls to limit rent increases. Finding a new home to rent has costs as well. Joe will have to find a mover or find friends to help him move to another home.

Sarah wants to buy a home to reduce rent risk. She has been looking at homes online and has found a capable real estate agent to help her. She does not yet know the price of a home that she can afford, because she doesn't know what amount of a mortgage a bank will approve for her to borrow.

Sarah decides that she needs to talk to a mortgage lender to find out what size loan she would qualify for, and, therefore, the price of the home she can afford. She is a first-time home buyer and knows that some lenders will offer incentives for first-time homebuyers, like waiving PMI costs, reducing closing costs, etc. She finds a lender who will finance 90% of her home price. Sarah will deposit 10% of the home price as a down payment, and the bank will finance the rest, which is 90% of the home purchase price. The 90% that she is financing is called loan to value or referred to as LTV.

Why do we need to know the down payment required? For two reasons:

1) The down payment amount *(10% for this loan)* will show Sarah the amount of money she must have in her bank account to pay for a down payment. She will also need money to pay closing costs to close on the property.

2) The down payment will be subtracted from the house price, and the resulting number will be the loan amount. Sarah will be qualifying to buy the home based on the loan amount.

Sarah is interested in a home that costs $350,000. What does this look like for Sarah? She wants to know how much money she must put down as her payment. She wants to ensure she has savings or investments to pay for the 10% down payment, plus closing costs.

Let's do the math and find out what Sarah would need for a down payment.

> $350,000 home price
> 10% down payment is 10% of $350,000, which is equal to $35,000 *(10% converts to decimal → .10 X $350,000 = $35,000)* Sarah will have to pay $35,000 as a down payment plus some fees at the closing table to buy the home.

Sarah has $60,000 in the bank to pay for the down payment and closing costs. So, she has enough money saved to afford the down payment on a home.

Sarah now asks herself what her monthly home payment will be. She wants to know if she can comfortably afford the home payment.

The home payment equals principal, interest, insurance, and property taxes as components of the mortgage payment. Let's examine principal and interest payments. PITI means principle, interest, taxes, and insurance – the full home payment per month.

First, let's talk about principal and interest. Principle is the amount of money you pay each month to the bank on a loan to pay down the balance of the loan. Principle balance is the amount you owe the mortgage company at a particular point in time. Interest is the payment you make to the bank each month for the privilege of borrowing the money.

Paying off a loan over time through regular payments that cover both principal and interest is called amortization. For a fixed-rate loan, let's assume Sarah is quoted a rate of 6% per year for the term of the loan. The loan is amortized, which means that each month, part of her monthly loan payment is used to pay down the balance of the loan. The balance of the loan is called the principal balance.

For example:

> On a $350,000 home, 10% down is $35,000.
> The home loan is the home price minus the down payment.
> $350,000 - $35,000 = $315,000.
> $315,000 is the loan amount.

We need some more information to calculate the mortgage payment.

Interest rate – The interest the mortgage lender quoted Sarah for the loan is 6% annually.

We also need to know the loan term. How many years will Sarah have to pay monthly mortgage payments? The lender tells Sarah that she can get a 30-year loan.

We now have everything we need to calculate the monthly payment for Sarah.

> 6% interest
> 30-year term loan
> $315,000 loan is the amount borrowed.

If Sarah's lender required private mortgage insurance also known as PMI, the PMI cost would be added to the loan payment. Other costs that may be added are home insurance costs and property taxes.

There are many apps on Google and Apple that calculate mortgage payments that you can use. It's easier than hand calculating the payment.

Search on the Internet or find an app for your phone that calculates mortgage payments. Most financial apps can calculate loan payments. Typically, we enter the loan amount or present value *(PV)*, the interest rate *(I)*, and the loan term, or N for the number of payments. Sometimes we also have to enter twelve as twelve payments per year. The following information is typical of the information you will need to add.

6 is entered as Interest *(I)*.

The loan term, 30 years, is entered as *(N)*.

The loan amount, $315,000 is entered as loan amount or present value *(PV)*.

Then, we need to calculate the payment. This is often listed as PYMT. We are trying to get the monthly payment, where the loan is a combination of principal and interest added together. Some apps are very easy to work with. Rather than showing the word, PYMT, an app might show a button called Payment or Calculate.

The principal and interest payment added together will be the monthly loan payment.

Principle + Interest = Loan Payment

We now solve for loan payment *(principal and interest payment)* = $1,888.58

Some lenders also will add property taxes and home insurance to the loan payment.

So, when we look at this payment, which includes taxes and insurance, you may hear or see them refer to it as PITI. This means principal, interest, taxes, and insurance. Let's estimate that Sarah will pay $700 per month in taxes and insurance. This amount may be added to her monthly payment by the mortgage company.

Sarah's total mortgage payment including taxes and insurance is:

Principal and Interest   = $1,888.58

Plus Taxes and Insurance = $700

Total Loan Payment   = $2,588.58

Sarah and Joe meet at a coffee shop to talk about their home purchase and renting.

Joe's rent costs look like this over five years. Joe asked his landlord about rent increases for each year that Joe would rent the home. The landlord told Joe that the rent charged per month would increase to $2,700 the second year, $2,900 the third year, $3,000 the fourth year, and $3,100 the fifth year. Joe's rent per year is shown below:

Joe's Rent Per Year Over Five Years
Year 1 - $2,500 X 12 months = $30,000
Year 2 - $2,700 X 12 months = $32,400 8% increase in rent from year 1
Year 3 - $2,900 X 12 months = $34,800 7.4% increase in rent from year 2 to 3
Year 4 - $3,000 X 12 months = $36,000 3.4% increase in rent from year 3 to 4
Year 5 - $3,100 X 12 months = $37,200 3.3% increase in rent from year 4 to 5
Total Cost of Rent for Five Years: $170,400.

In addition, Joe must pay renter's insurance to protect his belongings in the home from fire or damage. Most landlords will require that the tenant pay renters insurance. If you are renting, the insurance will be an additional cost to you. I strongly recommend getting this insurance to safeguard your belongings if the home is damaged or destroyed. You will want to file a claim to cover the cost of your furniture and belongings in these circumstances.

Sarah explained her cost for a fixed-rate mortgage over five years. Her homeowner's insurance and property taxes increased each year by a small amount, which affected her mortgage payment. An increase in taxes and insurance will typically occur each year.

Year 1 - $1,889 + **$700** Insurance and tax = $2,589 monthly X 12 months = $31,068
Year 2 - $1,889 + **$710** Insurance and tax = $2,599 monthly X 12 months = $31,188
Year 3 - $1,889 + **$725** Insurance and tax = $2,614 monthly X 12 months = $31,368

Year 4 - $1,889 + **$750** Insurance and tax = $2,639 monthly X 12 months = $31,668
Year 5 - $1,889 + **$780** Insurance and tax = $2,669 monthly X 12 months = $32,028
Total Cost of Mortgage for Five Years: $157,320.

Sarah's home and belongings are insured by her homeowner's insurance, which is included in her monthly mortgage payment.

When Sarah and Joe compare their home costs, Joe is paying $170,400 and Sarah is paying $157,320. Sarah is paying $13,080 less than Joe for home costs because she bought a home. She also learned she can write off the interest and taxes paid on the loan on her annual income tax return, which will save her money on her taxes.

The primary benefit for Sarah is that she knows her monthly payment of principal and interest is the same for the rest of the loan because she has a fixed-rate mortgage. She knows that her monthly mortgage payment will be more consistent. Joe will be paying more than Sarah by renting over the next five years. Joe decided, after talking with Sarah and seeing the difference in their costs over five years, that he would start saving for a home so he can lock in a more consistent regular monthly payment that he can depend upon each year.

It's a good idea to know what the loan payment is but it's even more empowering to know HOW to calculate the loan payment. Calculating the loan will help you know what your house payment will be and if it's affordable and fits your budget.

Consider taking these three steps if you contemplate buying a home:

1) Ask your lender what the current interest rate is for mortgages loans. The interest rate will vary daily. Some lenders will charge a lower interest rate for a loan if you put more money down, like 20% or 25%.

2) Check the home prices for the type of home you want. This will help the lender, and you calculate the estimated mortgage payment to see if it fits your budget.

3) Ask your lender to pre-approve you for a home loan. The lender will look at your credit score, income and your debt including other loans and credit cards to determine the amount they will loan to you. The maximum loan amount you can afford will determine the price of a home you can qualify for. This calculation is called the debt-to-income ratio *(DTI)*.

I have worked with home buyers who have their heart set on a particular home or neighborhood, but they do not know if the home's mortgage payment fits their budget. They are sometimes disappointed when the home they want will cost more in a mortgage payment than they can afford.

You may want to ask your mortgage lender these questions about how a down payment can reduce the interest rate you pay on a loan:

- What would my loan interest rate be if I put down 10%?

- Would I have a lower interest rate if I put down 20%?

- How about 5% down?

The lender may have a lower interest rate if you put down 20% versus an interest rate if you put down 10% or 5%. The lender may also have a first-time homebuyer program that may offer discounts on rates, fees, and closing costs if you qualify. As a first-time homebuyer, ask your lender about the first-time homebuyer loan programs they offer.

Another consideration is the term of a mortgage loan. You can save on interest if you take out a 15-year fixed-rate loan rather than a 30-year fixed-rate loan. A 15-year fixed-rate loan is a loan that can be paid off in fifteen years. The loan may have a lower interest rate than a 30-year loan. Also, when it's paid each month, more of the mortgage payment is used to reduce the principal balance. This helps the homeowner build equity in the home because the principal balance of the loan is decreasing more rapidly. The challenge with a 15-year loan is that the mortgage payment is higher than a 30-year loan and may be unaffordable for some people.

Another type of loan is a 5/1 adjustable-rate mortgage *(ARM)* or a 7/1 ARM. These loans start with a fixed mortgage rate for the first five or seven years. But then the interest rate and your mortgage payment increase after the initial five- or seven-year term. For example, after five years, a 5/1 ARM's interest rate can increase by 1% or the percent the loan documents state. For example, a 6% starting interest rate *(years 1 to 5)* increases by one percent to 7% in year six.

The initial interest rate offered for the loan may be appealing because it may have a lower interest rate than a 15- or 30-year fixed-rate mortgage rate. But the ARM interest rate may reset after the five or seven years and could have a significant impact on your mortgage payment after the initial term.

Another type of loan is an Interest-Only Mortgage Loan. With this type of loan, the interest payment could increase if the federal interest rate increases, which will affect the interest rate paid on the loan. When the loan interest rate increases, the required mortgage payment increases as well. If you pay the same mortgage payment as before, less of the payment will go to pay down the principal balance. More of the payment will go to pay interest. If you take out a loan like this, be sure to continue to pay the principal balance down as well as pay the interest amount due. Some home equity loans are interest-only loans. If the payment you are making does not pay down the principal balance as well as interest, your loan balance will not be paid down.

I know someone who was a big fan of interest-only loans. He refinanced his home using a home equity line of credit *(HELOC)* loan.

A HELOC loan requires the homeowner to pay interest-only, with principal payment optional. After an agreed-upon number of years, the homeowner must start paying principal payments. The loan interest rate will be reset based on a schedule. We will assume the interest rate on his loan resets every six months.

The risk of having this loan is that if interest rates increase, so will the minimum mortgage payment. At the time he took out a HELOC loan, the interest rates were averaging 3% per year. After thirty months, the interest rate had climbed to 7.5%. His mortgage payment climbed as well. I don't know how he managed this increase. If we assume he took out a $400,000 loan, he would be paying $12,000 in interest per year or $1,000 per month at 3% interest-only. At 7.5%, interest-only, he would pay $30,000 in interest per year or $2,500 per month! His payment could have increased by 150% *($2,500 - $1,000 = $1,500 increase per month!)*. Interest-only loans look inviting, but they are risky if national interest rates climb above the interest rate a borrower got when the loan started.

Let's see some examples of mortgage payments for various loans with different interest rates and a thirty-year term.

Let's assume the mortgage amount for each loan is $400,000. Let's also assume that each loan requires a 20% down payment. Most lenders will waive a Private Mortgage Insurance *(PMI)* mortgage fee if a borrower puts down a 20% down payment. The interest rates used below are examples. The mortgage interest rates offered to buyers will fluctuate daily for each lender. The overall economy will also affect interest rates on mortgages. Keep an eye out for mortgage interest rates and their movement up or down if you are planning to buy a house.

Fixed Rate Loans

15-year loan – 6% interest rate = $3,375 per month for principal and interest

30-year loan – 6.5% interest rate = $2,528 per month for principal and interest

ARM Loans

5/1 Arm – resets at year six – Loan interest rate starts at 6% for years one to five. It increases to 7% in year six which equals $2,661 per month mortgage payment in year six.

7/1 Arm – resets at year eight – Loan interest rate starts at 6.25% interest rate for years one through seven. It increases to 7.25% in year eight, which equals $2,728 per month mortgage payment in year eight.

Interest Only Loans

Interest rates float monthly or annually. For example, a loan interest rate starts at 4%. Each year, the interest rate can increase based on the federal market rates. This will increase the mortgage payment required from the borrower.

The 15-year loan has a higher loan payment because more of the mortgage payment is used to pay down the principal balance.

The 30-year loan has a lower payment than the 15-year loan and the payment is consistent every year and may adjust for tax and insurance increases.

The 5/1 ARM will adjust in year six, which makes the monthly payment in year six more expensive than the 30-year mortgage (*$2,661 per month versus $2,528 per month*). This loan may continue to increase after year six, because it has an adjustable rate. For example, the rate may increase to 8% in year seven, which would make the loan payment $2,935, which may be more than a homeowner's planned budget.

The 7/1 ARM will be more expensive as well at year 8: $2,728. And year nine it could increase to 8.25% which equates to a payment of $3,005 per month. Can you afford for your house payment to increase to this amount when you had an initial mortgage payment of $2,463?

The interest-only loan has a payment where you can choose to pay only the interest charged on the loan. The principal balance or loan balance does not get paid down unless you pay extra towards the principal balance each month. This means that your loan balance will not decrease if you pay the interest payment only. For example, if you owe $400,000 on a home loan, you will pay the interest and will always owe $400,000. Most mortgage payments pay the interest and principal in one payment. I don't recommend interest-only loans, because the homeowner will miss out on reducing the home loan balance owed on the home, if they make the minimum payment *(interest only)*.

Some lenders may promote interest-only loans to investors who want to buy a property, fix it up, and then flip the property in a short period of time. The investors want a low mortgage payment to pay while they prepare the house for resale. The lender may also promote this loan to people who want to buy a home and then sell it in a relatively brief period, generally less than two or three years.

Banks and mortgage lenders have different down payment requirements and rates for each percentage down payment. Some government lenders require a minimum of 3%. Banks may offer home loans if you put down at least 5% or 10%. Some banks or mortgage companies will ask for 20% down, and if you pay 20% down, they will waive mortgage insurance premium on the loan.

Mortgage insurance premium, also known as private mortgage insurance *(PMI)* on a loan, is an additional charge each month for lender insurance because the buyer's down payment was less than 20%. It helps the lender provide a safeguard for investment companies that may buy your home loan from the lender.

Ideally, you should look for loans that do not charge a mortgage insurance premium. If you don't have a down payment large enough to waive mortgage insurance premiums, an additional monthly mortgage insurance premium may be added to your monthly mortgage payment.

The private mortgage insurance *(PMI)* rate is usually between .58% and 1.86% of the loan amount, based on the buyer's credit score and other factors. The rate is multiplied by the loan balance and generates a monthly payment.

For example, if we use .58% as the PMI, the mortgage payment for Sarah's loan would be higher.

Sarah's total mortgage payment including taxes and insurance and PMI.

> Principal and Interest = $ 1,888.58
> PMI = $ 152.25
> *(PMI is $315,000 loan amount X .0058 = $1,827 per year/ 12 months = $152.25 PMI payment per month)*
> Taxes and Insurance = $ 700
> Total Mortgage Payment: $ 2,740.83

If Sarah's lender required private mortgage insurance, her monthly payment would increase from $2,589 to $2,741 per month. That's why it's important to work with a mortgage lender before you look for a home to buy to learn these nuances that can greatly affect your monthly expenses.

For residential rental investment loans, the required down payment may be 20%-25%. For US veterans, some VA *(veteran)* loans offer a zero-down payment, and the closing costs are financed into the loan.

Loan Calculation: Let's Do the Math

Before a buyer goes to a mortgage lender, he or she needs to know how much money they have and can put down on a home. Let's help Adam do the down payment math.

Adam wants to buy a house for $500,000.

How much is his down payment at 20% down?

To calculate a down payment, use multiplication:

$500,000 X 20% = down payment
$500,000 X .20 = $100,000 down payment

Adam will be making a $100,000 down payment to the lender to close on the purchase of his home plus closing costs.

Anna, the mortgage officer, reviews Adam's financial information and credit score, and tells Adam her company can finance his home. The purchase price of the home he wants is $500,000. The mortgage rate will be 8%, provided Adam puts down 20% as a down payment. He wants a 30-year fixed-rate mortgage.

What does this mean? How does Adam develop a good understanding of the numbers, so he can make wise financial decisions?

Let's figure out the monthly mortgage payment. We have the down payment plus additional loan costs in the bank.

$500,000 minus the down payment of $100,000 = $400,000 which is the loan amount.
$400,000 loan amount with an 8% interest rate and a 30-year loan term.

In a loan program or on a financial calculator, we enter:

Loan amount: $400,000

Interest: 8% fixed rate for thirty years

Term of loan: 30 *(thirty years, or 30 X 12 months = 360 payments)*

Solve for loan payment: $2,935.06

The principal and interest payment is $2,935.06 per month.

What is the mortgage payment if we added in property taxes and insurance?

Most, if not all, homeowners pay property taxes on their home. Property taxes are assessed and charged to the homeowner by the local and state governments. The taxes collected from homeowners and businesses pay for schools, roads, emergency services like police and fire departments, and other programs.

Homeowner's insurance is paid by the homeowner to repair or rebuild the home in the event of fire, damage, natural disasters, flood, and other emergencies that affect the home.

Buyers should shop around for a homeowner's policy by talking with multiple insurance companies. Comparing insurance and picking a policy that works for the buyer and has the best price will save money each month, as the insurance is usually paid as part of the mortgage payment.

Let's say the property taxes on this home are $4,000 per year. Adam found insurance for this home for $1,200 per year.

First, we add up the taxes and insurance numbers: $4,000 + $1,200 = $5,200 per year for both taxes and insurance.

Then we divide $5,200 by twelve months to get the monthly cost for taxes and insurance. We divide by twelve because we want to know the amount that will be added to our principal and interest payment: $5,200 ÷ 12 = $433.33. Now the $433.33 is added to the mortgage payment *(principal and interest)*:

$2,935.06 Principal and interest *(PI)*
+   433.33 Taxes and Insurance *(TI)*
$3,368.39 – principal, interest, taxes, and insurance *(PITI)*

Adam would be paying an estimated $3,368.39 per month for a mortgage payment.

Knowing and understanding your numbers and doing the math will allow you to:

1) Decide whether to rent or buy a home.

2) Choose a mortgage lender offering the best interest rates for your down payment.

3) Figure out the price of a home you can afford to buy.

4) Shop for homeowner's insurance and research property tax amounts for the home you want to buy.

5) Determine what you can afford for a down payment on a home.

Ask your lender about interest rates and terms of various loans that show you the cost of the loan, the interest rate, the loan term, and the estimated mortgage payment.

What Does APR Mean?

The lender tells you that the interest rate for your home will be 6% annually and will have an APR of 6.5%.

APR means the annual percentage rate. The annual percentage rate is the actual interest rate you will pay after the lender adds all the fees it charges to process the loan. Ask your lender about the APR for the loans it offers and the fees it charges to close a mortgage. These fees increase your effective interest rate and the cost of borrowing for the home over the entire loan term. Some lenders may offer lower fees and competitive interest rates, so shopping at several lenders for the lowest interest rate and fees is a good idea.

How to Get the Best Deal on a Home

Your credit score can greatly influence what you pay for a mortgage interest rate because it determines the interest rate you'll qualify for. Also, some people look for opportunities to buy when interest rates decrease, or homes are slow to sell, and this can result in lower prices for homes. Buyers can get better deals when the housing market slows down.

Key Money-Saving Tips

1) Shop for a mortgage before you find a home and find out what your monthly payment will be for a home loan to make sure you qualify for the size of loan you need.

2) Do the calculations to figure out what your down payment will be and how much money you will have to put down and the interest rates available for each type of loan.

3) You may have to pay for private mortgage insurance *(PMI)* in addition to your mortgage if you are putting down less than 20%. Ask the lender what it requires and how you can avoid the cost.

4) Avoid an interest-only loan. Your payments will increase when the national interest rate increases.

Chapter 10

Achieving a Healthier Bank Account Balance through Budgeting

"The most difficult thing is the decision to act, the rest is merely tenacity."

–Amelia Earhart

When I grew up, we took family summer vacations. We didn't have a lot of money, so my mom and dad saved money for the family vacation throughout the year. We had a Volkswagen bus, and my dad packed the bus to the ceiling with camping gear and food. I remember there were three small empty spots on the bus, for us kids to sit. The rest of the bus was packed up. I don't know if my dad was able to see behind the car with his rear-view mirror! We drove from Nevada to California with all our camping gear to the state beaches. Camping on the state beaches saved a lot of money because we didn't have to stay at a hotel, which was much more expensive, especially for our family of five.

We cooked at the campsite, so we saved money on meals, instead of dining out. I didn't know it at the time, but my parents were teaching us how to be scrappy, save money for trips, and spend wisely while on those trips. Through this approach, we could afford to experience new and exciting places.

One of the ways my family saved money was by looking for sale items in the grocery store. My mom compared prices between national food brands and the store name brand and chose the item that was priced less. My mom spent time comparing prices of food items and used coupons when available, so she didn't have to pay the full price for groceries.

In Chapter 3, we discussed a budget that the teacher put together to spend a government grant of $1,000 on a field trip.

In this chapter, we are going to budget for a vacation for family or friends. We will then budget for the end-of-the-year holiday shopping and back-to-school shopping. Lastly, we will create a personal budget so we can pay for our monthly bills and find ways to have money left over in the bank account.

The worksheets that are used in this chapter can be found in Appendix B.

Budget for Vacations

Vacations are a welcome change from our busy and stressed routines. It's smart to plan for regular vacations, whether a long weekend or a several week trip. Many people motivate themselves to save money for vacations when they can picture the place where they want to go. Some people spend money to travel to see relatives or family. Whatever reason you have, you can save for a vacation. Saving the money for the trip will make the trip more enjoyable because you're less likely to be in debt when you return home.

Let's first plan for a budget-friendly trip. The first step is to decide what you will do on the trip and how much everything will cost.

Planning a Driving or Bus Trip

This type of trip is the most economical, most of the time. Whether you drive a car or ride on public transportation like a bus or train, your cost will usually be less than if you fly to your destination, unless you're able to get reduced airfare. If you fly, you will need to rent a car unless someone meets you at your destination and has a car or other transportation. Also consider that if you drive to the airport, you will have to pay for parking there for the duration. If you need to take a ride to and from the airport, that is another cost to consider.

Let's plan a trip to visit a national park.

Questions to ask yourself when planning a trip:

1) What mode of **transportation** will you take, and how much will it cost to get there and return home?

2) Where will you stay for **lodging** when you get there, and what are the price options for the accommodations?

3) How much do **national park passes cost** for the day? Does it make sense to buy an annual pass if you plan to visit the park for multiple days?

4) How much will you budget for **dining out**, or is there lodging that will let you cook your own meals?

5) What other activities do you want to do? How much will they cost, or are there some free things to do that look like fun?

6) Are you planning to buy souvenirs? How much will you budget for the souvenirs?

7) How much will you budget for unforeseen expenses such as a flat tire or other car emergency?

Freda wants to take her family to Yellowstone National Park. Her family includes her husband, Alvin, and her son, Jeremy. She must create a budget for the trip, which will help her determine the money to set aside in advance.

Transportation

Freda lives within a five-hour drive to the park, and she has a reliable car, so she has decided to drive rather than fly to an airport and rent a car to drive to the park. Freda has estimated she will spend $600 on gasoline to drive her family to the park, drive around in the park, and return home.

Lodging

Freda looks at the lodging options. She doesn't want to camp, so she looks at hotels and motels. She finds a motel outside the national park that has a kitchenette and will fit her family of three people. The motel is less expensive than a hotel so she can save money on lodging by renting this motel room. She plans to stay three nights and four days. The motel room rate is $100 per night including taxes and resort fees. She can then budget $300 for the lodging. When you're pricing a room, always find out what the taxes and additional fees will be. Also ask whether there is a charge for parking the car per day. Add up all of the cost for the room, taxes, resort fees *(if applicable)* and parking so you will know how much to budget for lodging.

Entertainment

Freda wants to visit Yellowstone National Park for three days. The national park charges $50 for a weekly pass for her vehicle to enter the park. She looks online and finds a special deal where she can buy a three-day park pass for $40. She thinks this is a good deal because she did the math as shown below.

Freda saved $10 in park pass costs. $50 regular price minus $40 discount price = $10 in savings. She looked at her options and chose the one that met her needs and saved money.

Food and Meals

Freda plans to make sandwiches in the motel and take them into the park for lunch. She plans to visit the grocery store before she checks in to the motel to buy food for the family to cook and eat during the trip.

She plans to spend $200 on groceries on the trip. In addition, she has budgeted to include a splurge on a dinner at a restaurant with the family during the trip. For the dinner cost, she estimates will be $40 per person or $120 for the family. She budgets $120 for dinner at a restaurant during the trip. Freda will budget $320 for groceries and dining out for the trip.

Other Activities

Freda decides that the park visit will take most of the family's time during the trip, so she does not budget for other activities. She knows that after she enters the park, all the places to view the geysers, hot springs, and geyser basins are free.

Souvenirs and Extra Things

Freda wants to buy t-shirts with the national park name for the family. She budgets $60 per shirt to be safe. She expects the t-shirts to cost $40 or less but Freda also wants to buy some earrings that resemble a moose. So, she plans to fit the shirts and her earrings into the budget. $60 per shirt times three people = $180.

Plan for Unforeseen Expenses: The Emergency Fund

Freda has a credit card with a zero balance on the card. She keeps the credit card handy for unforeseen expenses, like car trouble or medical care if someone gets sick.

Freda has budgeted $500 in her savings account to pay for sudden expenses if she needs it on the vacation trip. Freda will carry the credit card with her on the trip. She can then use it for unforeseen expenses. Hopefully, she won't have any. If she does and she charges the unforeseen cost to the credit card, she can pay off the card when the payment is due with the $500 she has put into savings.

Here is Freda's budget for her national park trip:

Transportation	$ 600
Lodging	$ 300
Entertainment *(park pass)*	$ 40
Food and Meals	$ 320
Other Activities	$ 0
Souvenirs/Extras	$ 180
Unforeseen Expenses	$ 500
Total Budget:	$1,940

Freda plans to save $2,000 for the family vacation in the year before the planned trip. She rounds up the $1,940 to $2,000 to make it easy to remember.

How much does she have to save each month and put away into a savings account for the trip?

$2,000 divided by twelve months = $2,000 / 12 = $166.66 rounded up is $167 per month.

Freda will save $167 per month to save up for the vacation she wants to take with her family.

Freda saves her money every month during the year and saves up $2,000 for the trip. She and her family take the trip to Yellowstone National Park in June next year.

Freda returns from her vacation, feeling refreshed and happy. Fortunately, she did not have any unforeseen expenses. Therefore, she can keep the $500 she budgeted for emergencies in a bank account and apply it to next year's vacation!

Planning a Holiday Gift-Giving Budget to Reduce Spending Shock After the Holidays

Have you charged holiday gifts for family and friends on a credit card, and found that you were in debt after the holidays? You may have been trying to get out of holiday shopping debt for the next six months!

This section will help you plan holiday shopping by preparing a gift list and estimating the price of each gift to help you set your holiday shopping budget.

To start a budget, we need to write down all items we want to purchase and set prices for each item. Let's start with the Thanksgiving meal. Then we will budget for holiday shopping *(Christmas, Hannukah, general gift giving)* and create a budget.

1) Thanksgiving Dinner

2) Holiday Gift Giving

For a holiday dinner like Thanksgiving, we need to budget for the main course, vegetables, side dishes, dessert, and drinks. Let's say you have decided to have dinner at your home. You first need to determine how many people will be having Thanksgiving dinner at your home. Knowing the number of guests will help you calculate the quantity of meat, produce, bread, or stuffing to buy.

To fill in the budget more accurately below, take a trip to a grocery store and write down the price for the items you would need to buy for the meal. Then add up the cost of each *"item"* category below. The *"Total Budget"* will help you plan for the meal cost.

The budget may look like this:

Thanksgiving Item	Price
1) Meat or Main Dish	$50
2) Vegetables	$30
3) Side Dishes *(prepare or buy ready-made)*	$20
4) Dessert	$15
5) Drinks – your choice	$50
Total Budget:	$165

A few months or more before Thanksgiving, you may want to prepare a budget for your Thanksgiving feast and put aside some money to buy Thanksgiving dinner items when the season comes.

Another idea is to start buying items on your list that are on sale at the store in the months before the November Thanksgiving season arrives if you have extra money to do this. The items would be non-perishable food like stuffing mix in a box, canned vegetables, frozen food, etc. Buying the items when they go on sale will save you money.

If in November, before Thanksgiving, your budget comes up short of what you want to buy, think about asking guests to bring side dish items to the Thanksgiving feast that they cooked or prepared, which will add more food to the meal and save you money. Planning a budget and saving money for it will reduce credit card stress during a wonderful shared American holiday.

Holiday Shopping Budget

Holiday gift-giving can be a major expense each year, depending on the number of gifts you buy for others and the price of the gifts. I suggest that you create your holiday shopping budget in January or early in the year for December, so you can save enough money during the year for spending during the holidays.

In high school, I worked at a department store, Broadway Southwest. On Christmas Eve, the store would keep the part-time salespeople on the floor to ring up customer orders and send the full-time employees home to be with their families. I worked part-time, so I was one of the last cashiers in the store before we closed on Christmas Eve. About three hours before we closed, I saw a friend, Marilyn, rush in, spot me at the cash register, run over, and ask me where five or six gift items were located in the store. She had just started her Christmas shopping at 3:00 p.m. on Christmas Eve! I understood what *"last minute"* meant on that day. She looked so stressed out. I don't think Marilyn had planned a budget for holiday shopping or budgeted time in her schedule to shop.

Let's set up a holiday budget so we don't have to stress out like Marilyn. Below is a holiday shopping budget for a small family. The budget sheet may be longer than this if you're shopping for many relatives and a long list of family members, coworkers, and neighbors. Greg is planning a holiday shopping budget. Let's help our friend, Greg, develop a budget for his family and friends.

Below is an outline of the gifts Greg will want to include in the budget so he can assign a cost to each gift and develop a budget for his holiday spending. Greg's budget is shown in Figure 10.1.

Greg's Holiday List Options

1) Gifts for the Children:

   A. Number of children receiving gifts

   B. Maximum price he will spend on a gift

   C. Number of gifts each child receives

2) Gifts for Significant Other:

   A. Number of gifts he will buy for his significant other For your budget, it may include wife, husband, boyfriend, girlfriend, or partner.

   B. Average price of a gift

3) Extended Family:

   A. Number of people who will receive gifts

   B. Maximum price spent on a gift

   C. Number of gifts for each family member

4) Friends and Neighbors, Co-workers, Employees:

   A. The names of his gift recipients

   B. The maximum amount to spend per gift

   C. Number of gifts per person

4) Holiday Decorations and Meals:

   A. Set a budget for a holiday meal using the Thanksgiving list above.

   B. Set a maximum budget for decorating the home for the holidays, or if you're like me, you'll pull out the decorations from the closet from last year, dust them off, and display them again.

Figure 10.1 Greg's Holiday Shopping List Including Gifts, Holiday Decorations, and a Holiday Meal

Person's Name	Number of Gifts for him/her	Maximum Price per Gift	Total Budget for the Person
Child – Suzanna	3	$50	$150
Wife – Maria	2	$80	$160
Family – Grandma Ella	1	$30	$30
Neighbor – Missy	1	$20	$20
Coworker John	1	$30	$30
Holiday decorations	1 Christmas tree	$60	$60
Holiday meal	Total food bill	$95	$95
Total:			**$545**

Greg has a budget of $545 to spend on his family and friends for the holidays. He thinks he will start budgeting for the planned expenses starting at the beginning of the year in January, so he can start buying gifts and non-perishable food before the holiday.

Greg is smart because he has a list of gifts to buy that he prepared in January. He can now shop during the year and buy the items on sale rather than pay full price. This can help reduce his costs for holiday shopping. He may have enough money saved by buying items on sale, so that he can splurge on another gift or dinner out with his wife, Maria!

Your holiday budget may be larger or smaller than the budget above depending on the number of people on your gift list. You can use this chart and fill it in with the names of your family and friends to develop your gift giving list and costs.

Some friends who have large extended families say they use a gift-gifting exchange where each person draws the name of one family member and buys one gift for that person. Then the family could afford the gift-giving exchange.

You may want to watch *(and account)* for extra costs that pop up such as gifts for your child's teacher or white elephant exchanges, etc. How do you plan for these expenses? It may be a good idea to set some money aside for small gifts for these events. However, if you do not have the money to put aside for these items, then offering a greeting card or handwritten note will be a good gesture. If providing a gift at an event like a white elephant exchange is expected, and you do not have the money to spend, then pass on the event or say you are not participating in the gift exchange.

There will always be a gift you forgot to buy. Or you may be invited to a party or event that requires a hostess gift or side dish presented to the host or hostess. Sometimes, a co-worker or friend buys you a gift which you didn't expect to receive so you now have to buy them one. If you have budgeted for the holiday and have bought items on sale during the year, you'll have extra money left over to buy them a gift as well.

USEFUL INFORMATION: A white elephant gift exchange works like this: 1) people choose to participate, 2) the group decides on the maximum dollar amount to spend on a gift, 3) people each buy a gift and wrap it, 4) each person takes turns picking a wrapped gift from the table of gifts, 5) people can choose to take someone else's gift that has been opened or choose one from the table.

Back-To-School Shopping

If you have children, back-to-school shopping can be a time-consuming, frustrating task and can be expensive as well if you don't stick to a budget for the necessary items.

To create a budget for back-to-school shopping, include the following items:

1) School supplies – pencils, pens, technology items, notebooks, paper, binders. etc.

2) Clothes for school – shoes, pants, shirts, socks, coat, sweater, etc.

3) Other items the school requires – backpack, school uniform, etc.

To develop a budget, put each child's name at the top of the page, and on the left side of the page, show the items each child needs for school. Then estimate the cost of each item and add the columns. The totals will tell you how much you are spending on each child. See Figure 10.2. If the total back-to-school expense is greater than your budget, then cut back on the supplies or clothes. An X in the sheet below means that the child did not need the item, so it was not purchased. Some non-profit organizations offer free backpacks and school supplies for the kids who need them. Seek out these organizations for help if you need it.

Figure 10.2 Back to School Budget

Back to School Supply	Anna	Bart	Aurora
Pants	$40	$30	$40
Shirts	$20	$30	$20
Backpack	$35	X	X
Pens/paper, Technology	$25	$25	$25
Shoes	$45	$45	$45
Coat	$100	$100	$100
Sweater	X	$60	X
Total:	$265	$290	$230

The shopping list may differ based on the weather where the school is located, the school uniform policy, etc. Use this table and adjust it to suit your needs. Back-to-school shopping can be expensive, so put aside money into savings early in the year so you will have the money to purchase these items before school starts.

> ★ **Math Hack Secret** ★
>
> Your personal budget is the starting point to find out where you stand with your finances.

General Everyday Budget for Your Home

To budget for vacations, Thanksgiving, holiday shopping, or back-to-school shopping, these costs must be put into your personal budget. Your personal budget is the starting point to find out where you stand with your finances.

To create a personal budget, the first thing to do is to print out or write down your current monthly expenses. I suggest you use three months of bank statements using your primary checking account and write out the expenses on a sheet of paper or export the data from the bank website to a spreadsheet. Then it will be easier to look at three months to identify the bills that keep reoccurring each month.

Write down your monthly expenses, which typically include rent or mortgage payments; car payments; utilities like gas, electric, and water bills; and cell phone, Wi-Fi, and any streaming and subscription services.

Pay attention to your electric bill, natural gas or heating oil bill, and water bill costs. If you live in a hot or cold climate, the cost of these utilities will be higher in winter or summer. Make sure you budget a dollar amount that will cover your utility bills no matter what month you are living in. To do this, get the last twelve months of utility bill payments, then average them to get a number that will cover your utilities each month. For example:

Electricity Bill for 12 months: Finding the Average Electricity Cost

January	$ 65
February	$ 64
March	$ 70
April	$ 85
May	$ 75
June	$ 125
July	$ 300
August	$ 250
September	$ 130
October	$ 76
November	$ 65
December	$ 75

Total electricity costs for the year are $1,380. Divide by twelve months = $115 per month average electric bill.

Adding $115 per month to a monthly budget will cover utility bills for most months. If the utility bill in a month is less than $115, like February's bill, $64, you will have savings for that month: $115 - $64 = $51. You can save $51 in your Money Keeping Journal and deposit the money in a savings account. Doing this will build your savings and provide cash to pay for utilities in months when utility bills are high, like July, in this case.

Let's help Skinny Mina develop her budget. To start, she first writes down the bills or expenses that she usually spends each month to create a total expense list like the one below:

Expenses – Usual Monthly Costs – Skinny Mina (per month)

1. Rent	$2,000
2. Natural gas *(heating)*	$ 50
3. Utilities / water	$ 120
4. Car payment	$ 600
5. Internet	$ 80
6. Electricity	$ 200
7. Insurance	$ 350
8. Cellular phone	$ 85
9. Home expense	$ 400
10. Childcare	$ 800
11. Fuel / car maintenance	$ 400
12. Dining out	$ 120
13. Groceries	$ 400
14. Designer clothes	$ 500

Then she adds up her typical expenses to create a baseline budget. A baseline budget is her typical money spent each month, added up to give her the average expenses she has each month.

Her expenses add up to $6,105.

Next, let's write down her take-home pay from any of the following: paycheck, pay received as a 1099 self-employed person, pension pay, Social Security pay, or payment received from others. She said she earns a paycheck from the company she works for. She is paid $6,500 per month after taxes and other deductions. When doing a budget, always use take-home pay, which is what you'll have to budget and spend. This pay is the amount you will use to create a budget.

Let's subtract her budget from her net pay to get the left-over income, or the amount of money left after she pays the regular expenses.

$6,500 - $6,105 = $395

Mina has $395 left over each month after she pays her regular expenses. That amount left over can be used for saving for retirement, saving for vacation, holiday shopping, or something else. We may have heard the term, *"pay yourself first."* Mina wants to retire from work someday and have money to spend during her retirement. She can pay herself first by investing some of her money into a retirement plan. Mina thinks $100 per month will work for her but she should check with a financial advisor to develop a retirement plan that works for her desired retirement date. She can pay into her retirement using pre-tax dollars, which reduces the taxes she must pay the IRS during tax season.

> ### ★ Math Hack Secret ★
>
> Every six months, review your budgeted expenses and compare them to your actual expenses. You can find your expenses in your checking account and/or credit card statements. Adjust your budget and mindset so you can spend less than your paycheck each month.

Let's change the income that Mina receives and see how this affects her budget. Suppose she finds her dream job where she can do work that she loves. The only negative is that she will take a pay cut to take the new job. The job pays $5,000 per month after taxes and deductions. If her current budget is $6,105, and she takes a job that pays $5,000 after taxes, she would not be making enough money to cover her budgeted expenses of $5,000 - $6,105= -$1,105 *(budget shortage)*. What should she do?

Mina may want to consider reducing her budget, to make it lower than her proposed take-home pay of $5,000.

Mina decides to do the math to find ways to cut her expenses. What should Mina look at in her budget for possible spending cuts?

1) Clothing expenses – $500 in designer clothes per month. Does she need to spend that amount on new clothes, or can she reduce this budget by buying fewer new clothes, or shop for non-designer items of good quality?

2) Childcare – Although the childcare company provides decent childcare, are there other companies or non-profit organizations that provide good care at a lower rate? Will other parents share in the childcare by taking turns watching all the children? She may research other available options or ask friends or colleagues about childcare alternatives that cost less than $800 per month.

3) Rent – Is the place where she is renting a reasonable price for the neighborhood, or should she consider a different neighborhood that may have more economical living space? Could she share her space with a roommate and split the rent cost?

4) Utilities – Is there a less expensive cell phone or internet provider that is satisfactory? Is there a way to save money on electricity or gasoline? Is she able to carpool with other coworkers?

5) Home expense – What is included in the home expense category and is there a way to reduce the costs?

6) Dining out – Are there other options for dining out, like finding restaurants that are more economical? Or having potluck dinners with friends and family where everyone brings a dish?

7) Should she get a part-time job to supplement her income?

Mina has decided to go for her dream job and cut back on the following categories of costs: 1) rent: find a roommate to share the rent and split the utility expenses, and 2) reduce her clothes shopping to $100 per month.

New Expenses for Mina (half the cost for rent and utilities) and reduced spending on clothes:

Costs	Old	New
Rent	$2,000	$1,000
Natural Gas	$ 50	$ 25
Utilities/water	$ 120	$ 60
Internet	$ 80	$ 40
Electricity	$ 200	$ 100
Clothes	$ 500	$ 100
Total Costs:	$2,950	$1,325

Mina can save $2,950 minus $1,325 = $1,625 by making two changes, inviting someone she knows well to become a roommate and reducing her spending on clothes. It looks like she can go for the dream job, because her dream job's after-tax pay is $5,000 per month, and the new expenses after her cost-saving measures are only $4,480 (*$6,105 in old expenses minus $1,625 savings*). The reduced costs are in bold in the budget below:

1. Rent	**$1,000**	
2. Natural gas	**$ 25**	
3. Utilities / water	**$ 60**	
4. Car payment	$ 600	
5. Internet	**$ 40**	
6. Electricity	**$ 100**	
7. Insurance	$ 350	
8. Cellular phone	$ 85	
9. Home expense	$ 400	
10. Childcare	$ 800	
11. Fuel / car maintenance	$ 400	
12. Dining out	$ 120	
13. Groceries	$ 400	
14. Budget-friendly clothes	**$ 100**	
Total:	$4,480	

Mina will have $5,000 *(new salary after tax)* minus $4,480 *(new budget)* equals $520 money left over each month. She can see other areas to cut costs as well, like by reducing her home expenses or selling her car and getting a less expensive one. These measures would allow her to save more for her retirement, too.

The answers to these questions will be unique to your situation. After you write down the budget, you will be able to see what you are spending money on, and you may decide to reduce the spending so you can plan for other fun events, like vacations and holidays.

For budgets, including your personal budget, the budget amount may change from month to month because the bill may be a utility bill *(gas, power, water)* that fluctuates based on the season. You may also have a recurring cost like insurance, that you should put the annual amount in the budget and divide by twelve for a monthly budget. Adjusting the budget to cover the once-a-year expenses will keep you out of debt because you are living within your budget.

★ Math Hack Secret ★

If you are thinking about changing jobs or retiring and moving to a new area, look up the costs to live in the new area such as the income tax rate, property tax, other taxes on income, rent or home prices, medical insurance rates, vehicle insurance and licensing rates. Add the costs to your planned budget. Some places in the country are more expensive to live in than other places, so add up the costs to make sure your income covers the expenses with some money left over.

Key Money-Saving Tips

1) Create a budget for yourself. Add up your utility bills for a one-year period. Divide by twelve to give you a utility cost that you can budget to cover you for most months.

2) Every six months, review your budgeted expenses and compare them to your actual expenses. You can find your expenses in your checking account and/or credit card statements. Adjust your budget and mindset so you can spend less than your paycheck each month.

3) Plan ahead for holiday shopping, Thanksgiving dinner, and vacations. Start saving money for these holidays in January to have enough money for the holidays and vacation.

4) You will find many sheets for personal budgeting, holiday shopping and other worksheets in Appendix B of this book.

Chapter 11

Making Excellent Math Decisions During a Typical Day

"Do not save what is left after spending
but spend what is left after saving."

–Warren Buffett

Every day there will be opportunities to use math to make excellent decisions and keep more money in your pocket. Below are some math opportunities we may see every week or month:

1) You have a local newspaper subscription. You receive a bill for the renewal of the subscription. The bill provides two payment options: 1) pay three months in advance for the newspaper, or 2) pay one year in advance for the newspaper. Which option do you choose?

2) You receive a credit card bill for charges you made. Do you pay the balance by the due date or pay the minimum payment? How does paying the minimum payment compare to paying off the balance owed on the credit card? How does that affect your money?

3) You go to a fast-food restaurant and pay for something with cash.

4) You are baking cookies and want to double the recipe. How much of each ingredient do you need?

5) You pay for a gym membership. Do you pay $30 per month or pay twelve months in advance and get a discounted membership rate of $20 per month?

6) You need to buy bottled water packs. Are these packs a good deal?

Let's start with the first one, the newspaper subscription.

Newspaper Subscription or an Online Subscription

Let's say you currently subscribe to a newspaper, magazine, or an online publication.

The newspaper representative calls you and says that your subscription will be expiring, and if you renew now, you can save more money if you renew for a one-year subscription. They also give a choice of renewing for a three-month subscription. How do you decide which subscription is a better one? Ask yourself the questions below:

1) Do you want to continue reading this newspaper or magazine? If not, then cancel the subscription and save money for other purchases.

2) The one-year renewal rate is $200 for the year.

3) The three-month renewal rate is $65.

How do we compare a three-month subscription to a one-year subscription to find the best deal? We have to do the math to convert a three-month subscription into an annual subscription to compare the two offers.

Let's convert the three-month rate to an annual rate:

Three months is one quarter of a year.
So, one quarter of a year costs $65.

To calculate a whole year, there are four quarters in a whole year. So, we multiply the three-month cost, $65, by four quarters to make it a whole year *(4)* * 65 = $260

If you had a three-month subscription plan, and renewed it every three months, you would be paying $260 per year.

If you chose the annual subscription, you would be paying $200 per year.

Which subscription is a better deal?

The annual subscription is a better deal because you save $60 per year. $260 - $200 = $60 saved by choosing the annual subscription.

Credit Card Bill: Pay Off or *"Let it Ride"* and Pay the Minimum Payment Due

Let's say you bought the refrigerator from ACME Warehouse previously mentioned for $2,000.

You have a choice of whether to use your existing credit card or apply for a new credit card that offers zero percent interest for twelve months. A stipulation of the new credit card is that you make monthly payments toward the credit card balance each month. If you miss a credit card payment, your interest rate will increase to the interest rate for the card. The zero percent interest will go away.

Which is a better deal?

The current credit card features a 5% annual interest rate. The new credit card is charging 0% interest for twelve months, with no annual fee and no transaction fees.

Let's figure out how much interest you will pay. To do a simple math problem we multiply 5% *(the current credit card interest rate)* times $2,000 *(the price of the refrigerator)* to equal $100. This is the annual interest that you would pay to use the credit card. Each card has compounding factors, and you will be making payments on the credit card every month to bring down the balance and pay it off.

The 0% credit card will charge $0 in interest for the first year if you make a credit card payment every month.

If you can finance a large purchase with a 0% credit card rate, it's a better deal than financing a purchase with a credit card that has an interest rate that will charge you interest for every month the purchase is not paid off.

Go to a Fast-Food Restaurant and Pay Cash

I challenge you to bring cash along when you go out to buy something, whether it be a meal or some goods. Why? Because then you can get some practice in counting back change to yourself. Also, when you carry cash to pay for everyday things, you can see the money that you physically take out of your wallet and place into the hands of others. It's more eye opening to see your cash literally leaving your hands than when you swipe or tap a credit card into an electronic payment system.

> 66 It's more eye opening to see your cash literally leaving your hands than when you swipe or tap a credit card into an electronic payment system. 99

You see a great Mexican restaurant that has take-out orders. You order a burrito and a drink.

The total of the meal is $13.85. You look in your wallet and see two twenty-dollar bills, one ten-dollar bill, one five-dollar bill, three quarters, and one dime.

Your wallet has the money in it below:

   2 - $20 bills
   1 - $10 bill
   1 - $5 bill
   3 - $0.25 cents *(quarters)*
   1 - $0.10 cents *(dime)*

The burrito meal is $13.85. We want to pay for the meal using as much change as we can, so that we have fewer coins weighing down our wallet. To start getting rid of the change, let's look at what we have. We see that three quarters and a dime add up to 85 cents (.25 + .25 + .25 + .10 = .85 or 85 cents. So, we can use our change to pay for part of the meal. What about the $13 that we owe for the meal? We can use a $10 bill and a $5 bill, or we can use one of the $20 bills.

We give the clerk a $20 bill and the 85 cents in change.

What should our change be? Let's count up from our order.

$13.85 is the meal price.

When adding change as payment, we count back.

   13.85 - .85 = $13

So, from $13, we count forward to the $20 using smaller bills.

   From $13 to $15 is $2 dollars.
   From $15 to $20 is a $5 dollar bill.

So, you should receive change from the burrito shop of $7 *($2 + $5)*.

Making a Recipe and Doubling the Ingredients

As you probably know, for cooking, doubling the ingredients isn't as important as when you are doubling a recipe for baking. With **cooking**, the flavor profile might be different, or the ratio of ingredients might change if you use more or less of something, but you don't have to double *everything*. When **baking**, however, your result will often be a disaster if you don't use math to double or half a recipe.

So, let's double the recipe. The recipe is for four dozen cookies. We want eight dozen cookies. We need to be precise when doubling the recipe so that the cookies still taste good. Doubling means everything is multiplied by two.

Cookie Recipe

- 1 1/2 cups of all-purpose flour

- 1 teaspoon baking soda

- 1 cup *(2 sticks)* butter, softened

- 3/4 cup granulated sugar

- 3/4 cup packed brown sugar

- 1 teaspoon vanilla extract

- 2 cups *(12-ounce package)* chocolate chips

How do we double it? Most of the items are easy to figure out.

1 teaspoon of baking soda becomes 2 teaspoons.
1 cup of butter *(2 sticks)* becomes 2 cups *(4 sticks of butter)*.
3/4 cup of sugar is equal to .75 cup. .75 cup times 2 is 1.5 cups.
3/4 cup of packed brown sugar is equal to .75 cup. .75 cup times 2 is 1.5 cups.
1 teaspoon of vanilla extract becomes 2 teaspoons.

1 1/2 cup of flour – How do we double it? First, convert 1 1/2 to a decimal – 1.5.
Then double it, 1.5 X 2 = 3. Three cups of flour are needed to double the flour ingredient.

Before you double a recipe, make sure you have enough ingredients available.

Pay for a Gym Membership

Oren wants to join a workout gym to get into shape. The gym salesperson tells Oren the monthly membership is $30 per month. Or if he pays twelve months in advance, he will have to pay $20 per month.

Oren is not sure if this gym is the best choice for him, but he wants to try it out. He may be saving money by purchasing the month-to-month membership if he plans to cancel it prior to one year. If Oren decides after six months to change gyms, let's figure out how much money he would save.

The monthly membership is $30.

If Oren keeps the membership for six months, what is his cost?

$30 X 6 months = $180 for six months of gym membership.

Annual membership is $20 per month but he would have to pay for the membership upfront for a year in advance.

$20 per month X 12 months = $240 per year he would have to pay upfront to start his gym membership.

If Oren worked out at the gym for only six months, his cost would be $180 instead of an annual membership cost of $240. He could save $60 by buying a month-to-month membership if he planned to stay for less than a year.

What if Oren stayed with the month-to-month membership for a year but forgot to change it to an annual membership and was paying the monthly membership rate?

> The monthly membership is $30 per month X 12 months = $360 per year.

Oren would pay $360 per year if he did not change his membership to an annual membership.

If he changed his membership to an annual membership, he would be paying $240 per year *($20 per month X 12 months)*.

Forgetting to change the membership has cost Oren $120 per year in membership fees that he did not have to pay.

★ Math Hack Secret ★

For memberships and subscriptions, I recommend you write a reminder on your calendar to indicate when your membership and/or subscriptions are up for renewal. Then you can choose whether to renew the membership or subscription before it automatically renews or terminate the membership.

Bottled Water Saver Packs... Find the Best Deal

You go to a store to buy some bottled water. On the shelf is an 8-pack of bottled water selling for $7.

Next to it on the shelf is a pack of 12 bottles of water selling for $10, with each bottle having the same number of ounces as the first pack.

Which pack of water is the better deal? And which one do you want to carry home *(ha ha)*?

The first one, $7 is for an 8-pack, which means we divide $7 by 8 to get the price per bottle.

$7 / 8 = .875 cents per bottle. Let's round the number up to 88 cents.

The second one, 12 bottles for $10. We divide the price by the number of bottles:

$10 / 12 = .833 per bottle, so we will round down to 83 cents per bottle.

Which water pack is the better deal? The second one, with 12 bottles and a price per bottle of 83 cents is less expensive than the 8-pack of water at 88 cents per bottle.

Key Money-Saving Tips

1) Always compare prices of similar items when at the store. Don't assume the sale-priced item is the better deal.

2) Look at memberships to clubs or online sites and determine if the rate and length of membership suit you, or if there is a better deal somewhere.

3) Double or cut recipes in half to create the size of meal or cookies you need.

Chapter 12

Familiarize Yourself with Differences Between Traditional and Common Core Math

"Hide not your Talents, they for Use were made. What's a Sun-Dial in the shade!"

-Benjamin Franklin

This chapter is for anyone who interacts with children who are learning Common Core math.

Common Core math is included in this book to explain it to parents who might be struggling to understand the differences between Common Core math and traditional math.

As a child, I was in classes of between thirty and forty students. The teacher tried to teach us math and keep our attention so we would understand it. It was hard for her, with many kids squirming around in their seats and not paying attention. I was one of the students who fell behind in math, in part because I didn't understand why it was important.

I asked some people what they thought of math when they were kids. Some said they saw that the nerds knew math, so to be cool as a kid, they had to not like math. It was a social norm to dislike math for some kids.

Other people said they didn't understand the use of math in real life. They had to do math problems as a kid, but the teacher or parents didn't show them how to apply it to daily spending that would come up as they became adults.

They would ask, why are we learning this? How does it work in my life now? Why do I need it when I grow up?

When I went to school, we learned traditional math. Now, however, I have heard about other ways of teaching math that set up problems differently than I had learned. Parents have told me their kids learn math in a way that is very different from the math the parents learned as kids. They could not help their kids with Common Core math, because it didn't seem logical to them or consistent with the traditional math they learned.

It is possible that parents can teach their children WHY they are doing math problems, and why it's important to know math. You may encourage children to like math by taking them shopping and showing them how to compare prices for fun to save money. The children can compete with others by searching out and finding more deals than the others. They would compare prices and do the math to find the best-priced deals. They can help their parents save money on purchases and write it in the Money Keeping Journal their parents keep.

Common Core math method breaks down math into parts, so the children can understand how the numbers relate to each other. It claims to be a way to visually learn math to make math problems easier by using columns and rows to break up large numbers into smaller parts. It teaches various strategies to solve math problems.

For Common Core or traditional math, we want to add 37 + 26.

In Common Core math, you break down the 37 into 30 + 7, and you break down the 26 into 20 + 6.

Then add 30 + 20 = 50 *(the big numbers)* and then add up the small ones 7 + 6 = 13, then add the two results together 50 + 13 = 63.

In traditional math, 37 + 26 can be calculated by lining them one under the other and adding from right to left.

Please see Chapter 3 to review how to add numbers manually using traditional math.

Some children need to learn Common Core math for school. The addition and subtraction tables, along with the multiplication tables included in the back of this book, also provide a great visual for the kids to see how the numbers work when added or multiplied together.

What if we had to solve the math problem 365 X 450 = ?

A good way to look at complex multiplication is to make it a word problem and solve it. For example, let's use 365 to be the average number of days in a year. Let's also say we make $450 in income every day. As a word problem, we ask, how much income do we make in a year *(365 days)*?

One strategy used in Common Core math would require that we draw columns and rows like Figure 12.1 below to solve this math problem:

   365 X 450

In Common Core math, it would look like this *(see Figure 12.1 below)*:

Break down the 365 into 300, 60 and 5; and the 450 into 400, 50 and 0. Put the numbers at the top and side columns. Then multiply each number on the top and left side of the boxes and enter it into the box that aligns with the two numbers. For example, 50 X 60 = 3000, put the number 3000 in the box that aligns with 50 and 60 on the chart.

Figure 12.1 Common Core Math Diagram

Common Core math Calculation			
	400	50	0
300	120,000	15000	0
60	24000	3000	0
5	2000	250	0

Then after writing all of these numbers in the boxes, add them up, and carry the one to the next column.

$$
\begin{array}{r}
\text{1} \longleftarrow \text{carry the 1 to the next column} \\
120{,}000 \\
15{,}000 \\
24{,}000 \\
3{,}000 \\
2{,}000 \\
+ \quad 250 \\
\hline
164{,}250
\end{array}
$$

In the fourth column, 0 + 5 + 4 + 3 + 2 = 14. Will the column fit a two-digit number like 14? No, only one digit in the column, which is the 4, so we write the 4 in the right column and move the 1 to the top of the next column to the left.

In the fifth column, we add 2 + 2 + 1 + 1 (*1 that we carried over*) to equal 6. Then we add the last column to the left, which is 1, and move the one to the bottom. The answer is 164,250.

Traditional math, it would look like this:

$$\begin{array}{r} 365 \\ \times\, 450 \\ \hline 0 \\ 1825 \\ 1460 \\ \hline 164250 \end{array}$$

To multiply using traditional math, we are multiplying from right to left using six numbers, then adding up three columns. It's fairly easy to learn.

In Common Core math, we multiply six columns, then add six columns. We **have to** design rows and columns to put the numbers in.

In traditional math, we use three rows for the problem above, because the largest number is a three-digit number.

Each school teaches math with different techniques. I thought it was interesting to see how Common Core math calculates answers to math problems. However, I prefer traditional math calculations because they are easier to write down and solve. This book uses traditional math to solve math problems.

Key Money-Saving Tips

1) Parents can work with their children to learn how to use math to compare prices at the store to find the best deals.

2) Common Core math is a relatively new way math is taught in school. Traditional math is used by most people in daily life.

3) Common Core math was developed for children to help them understand how numbers work together.

Addition and Multiplication Tables

Math Tables - Addition

	1	2	3	4	5	6	7	8	9	10
1	2	3	4	5	6	7	8	9	10	11
2	3	4	5	6	7	8	9	10	11	12
3	4	5	6	7	8	9	10	11	12	13
4	5	6	7	8	9	10	11	12	13	14
5	6	7	8	9	10	11	12	13	14	15
6	7	8	9	10	11	12	13	14	15	16
7	8	9	10	11	12	13	14	15	16	17
8	9	10	11	12	13	14	15	16	17	18
9	10	11	12	13	14	15	16	17	18	19
10	11	12	13	14	15	16	17	18	19	20

HINT: The best way to memorize addition tables is to randomly pick a number from the top row, like 6, and pick a number from the column, like 5. Memorize the answer of the two which is 11. Another way to memorize addition is to pick a number on the vertical line, like

3. Then memorize the answers across the horizontal access starting with 10 and moving back to 1. For example, 3 + 10 = 13, 3 + 9 = 12 then 3 + 8 = 11.

Multiplication Tables – Times Tables

	1	2	3	4	5	6	7	8	9	10	11	12
1	1	2	3	4	5	6	7	8	9	10	11	12
2	2	4	6	8	10	12	14	16	18	20	22	24
3	3	6	9	12	15	18	21	24	27	30	33	36
4	4	8	12	16	20	24	28	32	36	40	44	48
5	5	10	15	20	25	30	35	40	45	50	55	60
6	6	12	18	24	30	36	42	48	54	60	66	72
7	7	14	21	28	35	42	49	56	63	70	77	84
8	8	16	24	32	40	48	56	64	72	80	88	96
9	9	18	27	36	45	54	63	72	81	90	99	108
10	10	20	30	40	50	60	70	80	90	100	110	120
11	11	22	33	44	55	66	77	88	99	110	121	132
12	12	24	36	48	60	72	84	96	108	120	132	144

To memorize multiplication tables, start with a row, like the 3 row, and memorize the answers across the columns. Start with 3 times 1, or 3 X 1, then 3 X 2 until you reach 3 X 12. Memorize one row at a time and then ask someone to test you after you memorize the row, without you looking at this chart as you answer the question. They may say, *"What is 3 X 5?"* and you memorized the answer and said 15. You will find out that it will get easier to memorize the tables as you move down to larger numbers, like the 5 times tables. When you memorize the 5 times tables, you will have already memorized 3 X 5 = 15, so when someone says, "What is 5 X 3, you can say 15.

I found some tricks I could use when I worked in local government and finance. Memorizing the 12 times tables is very useful. When you hear someone say your loan term is 60 months, how do you know how many years the loan term is? You divide 60 by 12 months in a year to get 5. This is a five-year loan. Most loans, but not all loans, give you the term of the loan in months rather than years. It's great to convert the term to years so you can picture the length of the loan.

Budget Sheets for Planning and Money Keeping Journal

Holiday Gift Budget Sheet

Add the individual's name to the sheet under Person's Name. Ideas of names would be the first name of family, friends, co-workers, extended family, teachers, neighbors, mail carriers, etc. Other names could be events like the White Elephant Exchange, book club holiday event, etc.

Write in the number of gifts you plan to buy for that person.

Write in the maximum price you want to spend on the gift. This will help you budget for the holiday season.

Multiply the maximum price per gift by the number of gifts to get the Total Budget for the Person.

Write in the amount of money to spend on holiday decorations, and an estimate for a holiday meal, if you have a holiday meal each year. You can use the Thanksgiving Meal Budget sheet to help you calculate a budget for a holiday meal.

Holiday Gift Spending Budget			
Person's Name	**Number of Gifts for the Person**	**Maximum Price per Gift**	**Total Budget for the Person**
Holiday decorations			
Holiday meal	Misc.		
Total:			

Thanksgiving Meal Budget

This sheet is used to plan the budget for a Thanksgiving or holiday meal, including birthdays and other gatherings of family and friends.

Item – Enter the food and drink you plan to buy.

Price – Set a price of the item at the regular price.

Sale Price – Challenge yourself to buy some items when they are on sale before the event happens. The items would be non-perishable food like boxed food, dry goods, or canned food. Savings from the sales price can be entered into your Money Keeping Journal.

Thanksgiving/Holiday/Birthday Meal Budget		
Item	Price	Sale Price (if bought on sale)
Total Budget:		

Back-To-School Shopping List

This list will help you find the costs of sending children back to school. Enter the child's name at the top of the page, and fill in the cost for each item on the left side, e.g., pants, shoes, etc.

Add up each column to get the total cost for each child. This chart can be used early in the year to estimate school costs. Then you will know what the costs are and plan to save during the year for back-to-school shopping.

Back to School Supply	Child1	Child2	Child3
Pants	$	$	$
Shirts	$	$	$
Backpack	$	$	$
Pens/Paper, Technology Notebooks	$	$	$
Shoes	$	$	$
Coat	$	$	$
Sweater	$	$	$
Total:	$	$	$

Personal Budget

The personal budget sheet below is used to estimate your monthly expenses and then add the specific expense like the actual power bill for the month. This sheet can be filled out each month so you can see where your money is going.

After-Tax Income – This is your paycheck or income after taxes are paid. Enter the number in the top right corner box.

Bill – the incoming bill you receive that you have to pay (*e.g., rent, mortgage, car payment, loan,* power *bill, groceries, gasoline, insurance, etc.*).

Average Expense – This number is a combination of twelve months of actual expenses from the prior year. Add up all the expenses for each category and divide by twelve. The number is your average, so write it in the average expense box.

Actual expense is the bill you received to pay that month for like that month's power bill, insurance payment etc.

Additional Cost Savings – This amount is the average expense minus the actual expense for the month. The number will tell you if your expenses are higher than average for the month. Wonder where your money is going? It could be that the expenses are higher due to the time of year (*utility bills*) or because insurance payments are due, etc.

Personal Budget for _____Date __/__/__			After Tax Income: $_____
Bill	**Average Expense**	**Actual Expense for Month**	**Additional Cost/ Savings Cost (-), Savings (+)**
Total Budget:			

Money-Keeping Journal

Use this sheet or create your own to keep track of items you bought and how much money you saved by comparing prices and choosing the lowest price or best price.

Money Keeping Journal for _____

Date	Store Name	Item Purchased	Reg. Price	My Price	Savings (Reg. price – My price).	Where Savings Deposited